Dreams to Reality

Also by Laura Haskins-Bookser

The Softer Side of Hip-Hop:
Poetic Reflections on Love, Family, and Relatinships

Dreams
to Reality
Help for Young Moms
Education, Career,
and Life Choices

Laura Haskins-Bookser

Illustrated by Jami Moffett

Morning
Glory
Press

Buena Park, California

YA
306.874
Hq
e.1

Copyright © 2006 by Laura Haskins-Bookser

A Student Journal
to accompany *Dreams to Reality*
is available from Morning Glory Press.

Library of Congress Cataloging-in-Publication data

Haskins-Bookser, Laura, 1952-
  Dreams to reality : help for young moms : education, career, and life
choices / Laura Haskins-Bookser ; illustrated by Jami Moffett
      p. cm.
  Includes bibliographical references and index.
  ISBN-13: 978-1-932538-37-3
  ISBN-13: 978-1-932538-36-6 (pbk.)
    1. Teenage mothers--United States--Life skills guides. 2. Teen-
age mothers--Education (Higher)--United States. 3. Single moth-
ers--United States--Life skills guides. 4. Single mothers--Education
(Higher)--United States. 5. Motherhood--United States. I. Title

HQ759.4.H39 2006
306.874'3--dc22

                                                      2005058090

MORNING GLORY PRESS, INC.
6595 San Haroldo Way   Buena Park, CA 90620-3748
714/828-1998   888-612-8254
http://www.morninggflorypress.com
Printed and bound in the United States of America

Contents

Foreword

A woman who has a child when she's very young is likely to feel excited and scared, happy and miserable, perhaps all at the same time. She needs her family's help, especially if she's a teenager. If she's lucky enough to have that support, she may still feel the gate to independence is nearly closed because of her dependence on her family. She has the choice of parenting, yes, but other dreams may vanish — dreams of college, a career, a home of her own.

Laura Haskins was graduating from high school, filling out college applications, and dreaming dreams of a wonderful future. Those dreams quickly vanished when she realized she was pregnant. No college for her. Only dead-end jobs in a desperate effort to support herself and her daughter. For several years, this was her life.

In *Dreams to Reality,* Laura tells us how she finally picked up those dreams, researched possibilities for people in her situation, and discovered that, yes, she could go to college. In spite of relationship problems, poverty, and the responsibilities of parenting, she could find her dreams and work toward achieving them.

Her story makes good reading. It's an absolutely absorbing account of a challenging decade in her life. Young

mothers will find it fascinating, whether they are single or
married. (Eighty percent of teenage mothers are single
when they deliver.)

But this book is far more than one person's story, no
matter how intriguing that story. Laura adroitly weaves into
her book not only tips and information about going to
college, as she did, but also information on the need for
early prenatal care, the possibility of placing a baby for
adoption, information about postpartum depression, how to
escape an abusive relationship, making and sticking with a
budget, earning money at home, importance of the father
declaring legal paternity, paternal grandparents' rights, and
much, much more.

The underlying theme of *Dreams to Reality* is motivation. Anyone can dream dreams, but to make those dreams
come true takes planning, research, and working toward
those goals *every day*.

This is no "Once I got motivated, everything went
smoothly" book. There are bound to be setbacks in
anyone's plans. Laura's story demonstrates possibilities in
dealing with those setbacks.

Certainly not everyone even wants to go to college.
Statistics show that only one percent of teenage mothers
earn a college degree by the time they reach 30. The author
provides information about community colleges, other job-
training opportunities, and suggestions concerning jobs that
don't require any college education. This is extremely
important information.

A valid question, however, is how many more young
mothers would continue their education if they knew they
had opportunities to do so? How many young moms have
heard from their parents, friends, even school counselors,
that their job now is to care for the baby? Of course it's
their job to parent well, but that doesn't necessarily cut off

all other opportunities. And that's the point of this book.

I founded and taught in a public school teen parent program for 16 years. I wish I had had *Dreams to Reality* for my students. I wasn't well enough informed about workforce preparation and college opportunities for my students. This book would have been an invaluable asset.

In fact, one of my former students, now in her 40s, told me recently that she had been on her school's college track her first three years in high school. She was editor of the school's yearbook in her junior year.

Eve was pregnant when she started her senior year, so she transferred to my class for a semester. After her son was born, she transferred back to her high school for her final semester.

No one, not her counselor nor any of her teachers, ever mentioned college to her again. It was as if she had dropped off the face of the earth as far as college planning was concerned. She assumed her college plans were out of the question. She had married the father of her baby, although the marriage didn't last long. She struggled for several years, married again, had four more children, worked very hard, and today has a beautiful family *and* a Bachelor's degree. She earned that degree by taking a couple of classes each semester even as she parented and worked. When her children were small, she ran an in-home daycare business. By the time they were in school, she had gained accounting skills, and began to work in the school district office.

Eve's story resembles Laura's in her ability to reach her goals even as she parented.

It might have been easier for Eve if she (and I) had been able to read about and follow Laura's guidelines.

Jeanne Lindsay
Author, *Teens Parenting Series*   December, 2005

Acknowledgments

I wish to acknowledge and thank these people who contributed to this book:

Emily Taggart and Gaby Mata for their longstanding friendships and encouragement to write down the details of my adventures. Having characters like you in my life has made making memories more fun.

Sonya Cirilo, one of the hardest working single mothers I know. You have wisdom in you that I am not sure you are even aware of. Thank you for sharing it with me.

Ms. Val, my first teacher, who retired this year. Your enthusiasm and positive spirit encouraged my lifelong passion for learning.

Jeanne Lindsay and everyone at Morning Glory Press, who read, reread and offered me direction, assistance, and guidance. Your recommendations and suggestions have been invaluable.

George and Lillian Haskins, my parents, for helping me to become self-sufficient and self-reliant. You let me be the mommy, and for that I am grateful. It was you that made me believe that going to college was feasible.

My brothers, Jason and Brandon, and my sister, Sorina, for making Faith know she is loved and part of a bigger family.

And especially Bradford Bookser, my husband, for his tireless support and encouragement, and for our children, Faith, Aliyah, and Brady, who keep me dancing.

Thank you all.

Laura Haskins-Bookser

Dreams to Reality is dedicated
to my daughter, Faith,
who has been remarkably patient
with me for nearly 15 years.
I use her motto as my inspiration:
"Forget regret or life is yours to miss."
Let's keep on moving forward, kid!

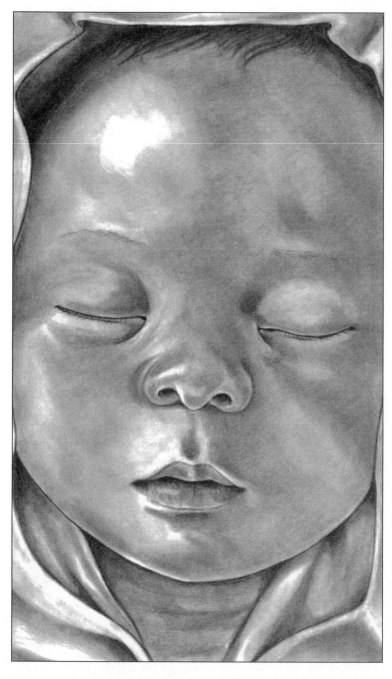

Introduction

So, one minute I'm taking the SAT, and looking through college catalogs when BAM! I got pregnant.

Okay . . . I wasn't exactly looking through college catalogs when *it* happened, but my life did change in the blink of an eye.

There I was: young and pregnant, a stereotype and misfit in a world of not-so-pregnant cheerleaders. My life veered into a different galaxy than that of my friends, whose lives suddenly seemed simple and carefree.

My world subsided into a whirlwind of smelly diapers and a powerful love for a 7-pound girl named Faith, who came into this world after fifty-six (yes, *fifty-six*) hours of labor. She was beautiful and perfect and, although I knew her creation was no mistake, I was unprepared for everything that being a mom required.

With Faith looking up at me with her big hazel eyes, I had a strong maternal urge to make a plan for myself. I wanted to give my child the best life I could. So I started formulating ideas in my head of how I was going to become a millionaire, and how Faith and I could live in a castle somewhere in the English hillsides, when all was said and done.

But those plans in my head bore about as much fruit as an apple tree in the desert. I was waiting tables, cleaning houses, and hoping against hope that one of the scratch-and-win lottery tickets I bought each week would let me live the fabulous life I knew I was destined to live.

By the time Faith was getting ready to start kindergarten, I hadn't done much of anything with my life. I went to work during the day, and sat on the front stoop in my crowded block each evening, watching my child play and listening to the bustle of my street. From the occasional brawl breaking out among the teenage boys who lived nearby, to the frequent loud arguments coming from the homes of our too-close neighbors, I was in the same hole I was in the day Faith was born, and I didn't know how to get out.

The only thing I did know was that I was never going to be satisfied living the way I was. I didn't want my daughter to be raised in the kinds of neighborhoods I could afford to live in. I watched too many young girls in my neighborhood saunter by, jaded already by the time they were in middle school. They used coarse language as a weapon in their constant battle against the hoots and hollers boys and men gave them as they walked by. I feared my daughter would also have to adopt such protective armor. I was five years into the parenthood thing when I said, "Forget the castle in England; I just want to live in a neighborhood that is safe for my kid."

This is where my story begins. For years I heard well-meaning family, friends, and teachers tell me that my dreams of college, a demanding career, and traveling were not realistic goals for a single mother. I assumed that they were right, and for years I struggled to pay the bills with my dead-end jobs. A fateful encounter with an acquaintance changed my mind, prompting me to make a list of ambitious goals that I planned to achieve with my child by my side.

I learned the hard way how to combine being a good parent with being a capable student, a reliable employee, and a safety-conscious world traveler. I now want to share the information I learned with other young moms who have the desire to break away from some of the stereotypes associated with being a single and/or young mother.

Every young woman who finds herself pregnant when she is unprepared for it will have to choose a path for herself. Each mother's dreams and goals will be different than mine, and different from each other's, but the key elements of *believing in yourself* and *setting goals* to reach your dreams will be the same. That is the focus of this book.

1

Pregnant?
Now What?

*T*he day I got pregnant was the day I finished my college applications. I clearly remember being at a small get-together that night and telling a friend there that I had just finished filling out my paperwork. He raucously told me, and the entire room, that I needed to celebrate the occasion. I wasn't a drinker, but that night, laughing and partying, I had some alcohol. Well into the evening, it was obvious I had too much to drink.

The next morning I woke up in a basement and wasn't sure how I got there. As I looked over and saw my date snoring in the bed, I remembered the laughing, partying, kissing, and eventual car ride that led me to his grandmother's house, where I now stood frantically rushing to get dressed and go home.

I was horrified! I wasn't "that type of girl." I was embarrassed and swore I would never let myself end up in that situation again. I pretended that the night didn't happen, and I threw myself into preparing for school. I started looking for a job so I could work while I was in college.

Weeks later, when I didn't get my period, I was distraught. I realized immediately that I was pregnant. I called my boyfriend and told him that I thought I was pregnant. I went to his dad's house and took a pregnancy test. When it came back positive, he punched a hole in the wall. *I knew it was the start of a wonderful relationship.*

I immediately thought about my options. I was torn between feeling afraid, amazed, and upset over the little person growing inside me. I didn't think I was old enough, mature enough, or capable enough to have a baby, but I knew my only choices were: abortion, adoption, or keeping the baby.

I liked children and always figured that one day I would be a parent, but this was not the way I imagined it happening. I was worried about where I would live, and about the problems I would have with my child's father. I didn't know what to do about money, and had no real job skills. I had only held low paying jobs, like delivering newspapers and baby-sitting.

My first thought was that I had to make the problem go away. I was a "good girl," and I didn't want people thinking that this represented who I was. I didn't want my family and my church to think I was some wild and promiscuous kid. I thought, "I will have an abortion and never tell anyone anything. No one will have to know. I can still go to college next fall and live my life like this never happened."

Days later I looked in the phone book for abortion

clinics and found one that wasn't too far away. I woke up early the next Saturday morning and took a bus to the clinic. The building seemed normal, not at all what I envisioned for an abortion clinic. I don't know what I was expecting, but it seemed like a regular doctor's office.

I went to the receptionist and told her that I wanted some information because I was pregnant and was considering having an abortion. She told me to wait, and that a counselor could talk to me if I wanted. I sat down, suddenly feeling hot and faint. I started to think about all my years in Catholic school, and of the Pro-Life rally I attended with my youth group the year before. I had been so certain then that abortion was wrong.

Suddenly it dawned on me how quickly I was able to see the other side of the argument. Now I knew why women had abortions. What kind of mother could I be to this helpless baby? How could I have a child knowing that I would be bringing her into poverty? How could I be a mother when I had never even become a real adult yet?

I felt nauseous and began to sweat all over. I thought about a conversation I had with the priest at my church. He told me that over the years he's learned that "God doesn't make mistakes; people make mistakes and then blame them on God." Even though I could see the other side of the argument for abortion, I wasn't okay with it. I got up to leave when a counselor came out and called my name. "Laura, I can see you now."

Instead of walking out of the clinic, I went into the office with the counselor. She seemed nice and genuinely concerned at how upset I was. She asked me about my situation and why I decided to come to the clinic. I told her I got pregnant by someone that I hadn't been dating very long, and that what I did know about him was that he was not really the "daddy" type. I told her I was raised Catholic, and always felt that abortion was wrong, but I had been thinking about it because I didn't know what else to do.

She asked me why abortion still seemed like an option for me, if I thought it was wrong. I told her that I just wanted all my fear to go away. I didn't want to tell my parents, and I didn't want to ruin my or the baby's father's life. She gave me some pamphlets and told me that I had a huge decision to make. She wanted me to read about all of my options, and to think about it for a few days before deciding.

That night I read the pamphlets and went to bed to a fitful sleep. I had a dream that I was in the park walking through a big field of pink and white flowers. Sitting in the middle of the flowers was a baby girl dressed only in a diaper. She was sitting up and smiling at me, and I felt happy. Then the baby laughed and said, "Have faith!"

I woke up and felt certain that the baby I was carrying was a girl. Up until then I had pretty much thought of the baby as an "it." Now I knew in my heart that I was having a girl, and that changed things for me.

I thought, "I am going to have a baby. There is a baby inside me, not an 'it'." I decided at that moment that I was going to keep the baby. I was scared, but I felt that it was the only choice I would be able to live with. Now I had to face the consequences of my choice.

Maggie Chose Adoption

I know I could've had an abortion, and it would have been easier, but I didn't. I knew I was having a baby, and I just couldn't see ending the pregnancy and pretending the baby never existed. Instead, I thought about what I wanted to do for three months before I told anyone. I went on the Internet and read about adoption before I sat my family down and told them I was pregnant. They weren't supportive when I told them that I was going to place the baby for adoption, but eventually they realized that I had thought hard about my choice, and accepted my decision.

I wasn't always confident in my choice. I wasn't sure that a baby who was half-black and half-white would have a good chance of being adopted by a couple. If the baby would be kept in foster care or something, then I wanted to raise him myself. But, if the baby could be adopted right away, then I would let a family who really wanted a baby have a chance to raise my child as their own.

I called an adoption agency. They told me that they had many couples that just wanted an infant and didn't care if it was a mixed race baby. They told me that I was the one who could pick from the couples. I was relieved in a way that I could choose my baby's parents!

I chose a couple that had a white father and a Hispanic mother because they seemed to be "right," and I thought that the baby might look like it fit with them.

I was in labor for 22 hours and gave birth to a tiny 6-pound 2-ounce baby boy. When I saw him, I couldn't believe I was going to give him away. I was so *tired from the labor and so emotional, I just wanted time alone with him.*

I held him and for some weird reason I wanted to breastfeed him, but the nurse told me that if he was being adopted it might be better not to. (I learned later that some birthmothers do breastfeed their baby a few times before releasing for adoption.)

I held him for like an hour, just watching him sleep, and I kept telling everyone to leave me alone. My mom was worried I had changed my mind and kept trying to come in the room with me. But all I really wanted was a little time to look at him and kiss him and see what he felt like.

I didn't change my mind. I signed the papers giving him to the couple I chose. I wrote them a long letter telling them that this was the hardest thing I ever had to do. I trusted them to be good parents, and to let me have pictures and letters like they promised.

They named him Anthony, and they kept their promise to send me pictures and letters. I even got one video from when he was learning to walk. He is almost three now, and I already have a big photo album with his pictures in it. If I saw him on the street I would know him right away, and that makes me feel better.

I get depressed sometimes, but I just finished my first year of college. I know I couldn't have done that right now if I had a baby.

Anthony was not a mistake. He was born through me to be the child that his parents always dreamed about. I know that now, even though I always think about him, and I feel torn about what I did. In the end, however, I know it was the right decision for me.

Did You Know . . .

Finishing high school is vital?

*I*t seems obvious that teen mothers need to finish high school to get a job that pays decent wages. Many teen mothers, however, who drop out of high school during their pregnancy will not return to get their diploma. Others leave school when life becomes too hectic after the baby comes, while others feel too removed from high school to want to return.

It is fortunate that there are now laws to protect pregnant students, as well as alternatives to traditional high school for teen mothers. These alternatives include schools that are specifically for pregnant and parenting teens, or special classrooms within traditional high schools that cater to the needs of pregnant girls and teen mothers.

Home-schooling/independent study may be an option for students who have the drive to work independently at home. Home-school laws vary from state to state, so check with your school district.

If you have not graduated from high school, are pregnant or have had a baby, it is vital to you and your child's future that you get a high school diploma. If not, you are very nearly choosing that you will live a life of poverty. More than 90 percent of the people who do not get a high school diploma live below the poverty line.

To get information about schooling options as a pregnant or parenting teen, call your local school district office and ask questions. Decide on which option will work best for you, and then make one of the best parenting choices you can make: be an educated mommy!

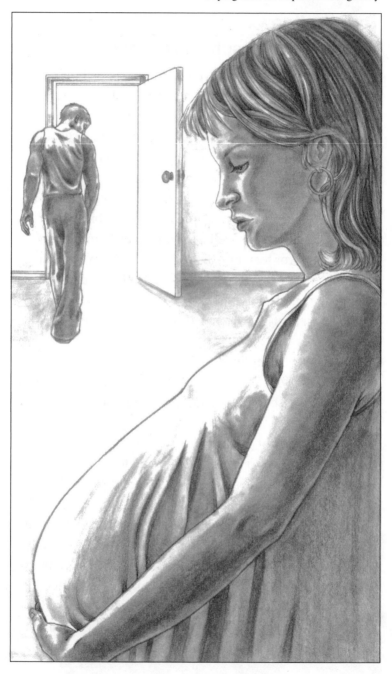

2

Coping with an Unplanned Pregnancy

I told my parents even before I confirmed my pregnancy with a doctor. They were disappointed in me, but still supportive of my decision to keep and raise the baby. They didn't yell or cry or do any of the things I had imagined they would do. They just had question after question.

"You're having a baby? How are you going to do that?"

"Who is the father? What is he going to do about this?"

"Who are his parents? Do they know you're pregnant?"

They were sad that I got pregnant the way I did, and I know they were in shock. They let me know that although they supported my choice to raise the baby myself, I would need to look for a job and find my own place for the baby and me. They told me that they wanted to be grandparents, not parents to the new baby.

At first, I couldn't believe that they weren't going to let

me live at home. I thought, "I've never had my own apartment, so how am I going to get one and have the money to
keep it while I'm pregnant? How will I work after the baby
is born?" I had expected that since I wasn't going to
college like I planned, my parents would let me live
at home.

When the reality hit me that I was going to have to do
this by myself, I knew I would need to hurry and get a job
before my belly started showing. I started to figure out how
much I would need for rent (including initial deposit), bills,
and baby things, and then I began looking for work.

At first I told my potential employers that I was pregnant, but after seeing how quickly they closed the door on
me, I began to hide my pregnancy during interviews. I did
frequent baby-sitting while I was job-hunting so I could
start saving money.

I also began using the library as my sanctuary. I didn't
know much about infants, so I started reading every book
on child development that I could find. I was sure that if I
had all the right information, I could learn to be a good
mother. I read about my body and the changes that would
develop during pregnancy. I read about childbirth for the
first time and, after seeing pictures of a woman delivering
her baby, I was so terrified that I cried myself to sleep.

However, the most frightening things I read were books
with statistics on very young parents. I read that less than
half of all teen mothers graduate from high school, and
only a little over one percent of young single mothers ever
get a college degree.

These statistics reflect the dire reality of their financial
situation. As you can imagine, it's not usually a very pretty

picture. Nearly eighty percent of unmarried mothers, under the age of 21, end up getting some form of aid from Social Services, even if it is just aid for medical care. And if she's under 18, she can't even apply for TANF (Temporary Aid to Needy Families) on her own. Being 18 gave me more options than I would have had a year earlier.

I became a statistic even though I eventually found a job as a maid and moved out of my parent's house. I was a high school graduate, four months pregnant, who had given up my dream of going to college in exchange for washing other people's stinky underwear.

I was tired all the time, and discouraged that my money went only to bills. None was left over for the cute baby items I saw everywhere. When I realized that minimum wage wasn't enough to pay all my bills, I had to go on public assistance to get medical benefits to use for my prenatal visits and delivery. I was embarrassed and depressed by my situation.

I became desperate to make everybody believe that the baby's father and I would make things work. I thought that was what was "supposed" to happen. I would get angry if anyone implied otherwise. But I knew that I was on shaky ground in my relationship, and I accepted things that I shouldn't have out of fear that he would leave.

I tried to force him to grow up and become responsible. I told him that he was going to be a daddy, and he needed to earn some money to help pay the bills. He didn't say it out loud, but he let me know in subtle ways that he wasn't that interested in family life. He continued to live his life like any other teenage guy.

He told me that he was a musician, and he wanted to follow his dream of becoming a superstar. In the meantime he was living a life-style that included drugs and drinking. I ignored the problems and pretended that everything was great. I convinced myself that one day we would have a big house, complete with a white picket fence and fluffy dog.

When I was several months pregnant and had not yet seen a doctor, his mother paid for my first doctor's appointment. My healthy pregnancy was confirmed in the form of a black and white ultrasound of a little peanut-headed baby. I was so excited to see a living baby inside me!

I begged the baby's dad to find a job to help with my bills. He got a job washing dishes and moved in with me but, with our two small incomes, money was extremely tight. He lived with me, and handed over a portion of his paycheck, but he still came and went whenever he felt like it. I often lay at home waiting for him, tired, bloated, and angry.

I began to feel resentful of his freedom. We *both* were having a baby, and I wondered why I was the one who was left to take care of everything at home. I wanted and needed his help, but he was not ready, willing, or able to be the person I needed him to be. The reality was, even before my baby was born, I knew that her father and I were from two different worlds. I was so caught up in preparing for the baby, I didn't dare dwell on it.

I learned pretty quickly that there were many responsibilities in living without my parents' help. I couldn't afford the things I needed. My parents bought me Faith's stroller, clothes, and diapers. My best friend, Emily, brought me a giant oven-sized box full of diapers, lotions, and other baby care items. Other friends brought me gifts, too, but I had to get almost every other baby item I owned from secondhand stores because I couldn't afford them new.

Emily was the person who helped me keep my sanity. She remained a good friend during my pregnancy. When virtually every other friend I had disappeared into the woodwork, she would gladly pick me up to go for a ride or to walk the mall. She helped me feel okay about the baby coming, and listened to me talk about all the hard things I was going through. She always had a joke or funny story to tell me, and didn't treat me differently because I was pregnant. Her mother was kind to me, and was not judgmental like some of my other friends' parents.

I appreciated her friendship so much because on a daily basis I lived in a scary survival mode. I never could live paycheck-to-paycheck, because my paycheck didn't stretch far enough for that. I was drained from my physical changes, and mentally worn out from my relation-ship. I was under incredible stress from living with so many worries.

As a result of my troubles, I began having complications with my pregnancy. The doctor recommended bed rest, but I knew I couldn't afford it. My blood pressure skyrocketed. Pennsylvania summers can be brutal, and by July, I was walking two miles to and from work in 90-degree heat. I was not taking care of myself, and began having dizzy spells that I hid from both the doctor and my family.

I finally had to quit my job when I woke up alone in my apartment, face down on the floor, and realized that I had passed out. I got in the shower and doused myself in cold water, then positioned the fan directly on me. I was having

strong contractions, but wasn't due for another two months.
I got so scared that I called Emily and asked her to take me
to the hospital.

The ER staff gave me an IV to stop the contractions, and
called my regular doctor. The doctor warned me that I had
high blood pressure and was anemic. He told me that if I
didn't go on bed-rest immediately that I would probably
deliver a premature baby who was sick and might have
lifelong complications.

So I relied on my boyfriend to take care of the bills. He
took on a new role, suddenly helping around the house and
talking about getting married. I was on an emotional roller
coaster. I had high swings where I fantasized about being
married to him. I also had low swings where I was depressed, angry, and resentful. During those times, I swore I
would die before becoming his pregnant bride. In the end, I
gave birth as an unmarried teen mother in a shaky and
volatile relationship.

For more information about the things you need to
know before moving into your own apartment, see
*Moving On: Finding Information You Need for Living
on Your Own* by Pollock (Morning Glory).

Pregnant? See Your Doctor *Now!*

I know now that I should have seen a doctor immediately after I realized I was pregnant. If I had, perhaps I could have avoided some of the health problems I had later in my pregnancy.

Anyone, young or older, who thinks she might be pregnant, needs to have her pregnancy verified as soon as possible. If she might consider an abortion, the earlier she can be sure this is her choice, the safer the procedure will be.

Early prenatal health care is extremely important for all pregnant women, and even more important for very young moms. Seeing a doctor during her first trimester gives her a better chance of delivering a healthy baby. The doctor will check for any possible high-risk condition, prescribe appropriate vitamins, offer advice on nutrition and the dangers of smoking, drinking alcohol, or taking drugs during pregnancy.

Teenagers, especially, may need to change their diets rather radically when they're pregnant. French fries and sodas don't build healthy babies. Milk, protein foods (meat, beans, eggs, cheese, etc.), fruits and vegetables, and whole grain foods are vital baby-building blocks.

Drinking, smoking, and drugs are likely to harm a fetus. Tragically, the most dangerous time for the mother to drink or take drugs is during the first two months of pregnancy, a time when she may not realize she is pregnant. Getting drunk even once can harm the baby at this point.

Taking childbirth preparation classes is also important. You may find free or low-cost classes through your adult school or hospital. As I mention later, I was able to attend only two of my classes. I'm quite sure I could have handled my labor and delivery better if I had been trained in relaxation and other techniques of prepared childbirth. If my boyfriend had been trained in these techniques, he might also have been able to help me cope with my long and difficult labor.

You need a coach who will take the classes with you. If you're with the baby's father, he may be your obvious choice. If you aren't with the father, or don't want him in the labor and delivery room, perhaps your mother, a friend, or even your father would like to be your coach.

*W*hile you're still pregnant is the time to think about birth control. Of course you don't need it right now to prevent pregnancy (although it's always safer to use a condom if you're having intercourse to protect you from STIs [Sexually Transmitted Infections]). Now, however, is the time to be thinking about the kind of birth control you'll use after you deliver. Will it be abstinence, the pill, the patch, or . . . ?

Talk with your doctor about the various kinds of birth control. If you choose the pill, will you remember to take it every day? Would the hormone injection that you must repeat every three months be a better choice? Or the patch that you replace each week? Or perhaps the contraceptive implant? These are some of your options, and new methods of birth control continue to be developed.

If, in spite of good planning, unprotected sexual intercourse occurs, see your healthcare provider for emergency contraception. This medication can prevent pregnancy if taken within 72 hours after intercourse.

You might want to ask your healthcare provider for a prescription for emergency contraception so you'll have it on hand if necessary. In some states you can buy it without *a prescription and/or online, <www.NOT-2-LATE.com>*

If you'll be breastfeeding your baby, this may affect your choice of birth control methods during the first months after delivery. (Do not count on breastfeeding to prevent pregnancy.) Some methods may interfere with milk production while others won't.

Whatever your decision, remember that you could get pregnant two weeks after delivery. You probably don't want that to happen — for your sake, and especially for this baby's sake, who needs you, and who won't want to share you with another baby in the next two or three years.

Did you know . . .

Declaring paternity is important?

*M*ost studies indicate that fathers, young or old, want to be involved with their children. But many young dads are fearful or just don't know how to parent a child. In addition, they may have to face negative reactions from the mother of their child or the parents of the mother. Many young fathers report their lack of involvement with their child is because of the resistance they get from the child's mother.

Unmarried fathers have feelings and needs. They also may be confused about their role as a parent. They need hope and encouragement to help them see a future in their child's life. If the father doesn't live with the child, and isn't given the role of taking care of his child on a daily basis, it is harder for him to bond with his infant.

Encourage the father to hold, cuddle, and take care of the baby. Just like unmarried mothers, unmarried fathers can be good and loving parents. But if they have to deal with a negative situation every time they want to see their child, they may decide that their lives are easier without the mother and child.

Your child is not yours alone. Respect the father's right to parent his child. If you're not married to your child's father, whether or not you're in a relationship with him, be sure he declares legal paternity of the child. This means you both sign legal papers stating he is the father of your child. If you don't, your child might not be able to claim Social Security, insurance, veterans' and other types of benefits through him.

The easiest way for him to declare paternity is in the hospital after your baby is born.

If he isn't willing to sign the paper showing that he's the father, get a lawyer, go to your local courthouse, or visit the Department of Social Services to get information. You can get help in filing the appropriate paperwork. The local District Attorney's office may help you with your paternity action even if you are not receiving public assistance.

Paternity orders can be enforced with a DNA test. This involves taking a blood sample from the baby after s/he's born, and from you and the presumed father, followed by genetic testing of the blood.

Once a father has claimed paternity (legal fatherhood), even if he didn't initially respond to the pregnancy the way you had hoped, he may change his mind. If he realizes that he can see his child and be a part of his or her life with encouragement from you, your child will be the one to benefit from having two parents to love and legally provide for his or her needs.

Believe it or not, you may have a strong influence over whether or not your child's father will continue a relationship with his child as time goes on. A father who is involved in the early care of his child, and is encouraged by the child's mother to spend time with that child, is more likely to *continue* a relationship with his child. In addition, if your parents encourage your child's father, and have a positive relationship with him, he will be more committed to staying involved.

For more information, read "Why Dads Are Important." See the Appendix, pages 165-166.

3

Those Early Days with Baby

*F*or some people there is nothing more terrifying than going into labor for the first time. You know what is about to happen. You will be squeezing another human being out of your body, in what seems like an almost impossible way.

I was on bed rest, thus only able to attend two of my childbirth classes. When I went into labor, I suddenly realized how important those classes were. I was not mentally prepared for labor to begin. I was panicked, and I had no coping techniques to fall back on. I hadn't learned what to expect, or how to calm myself.

Not only did I go into labor, I went into denial, too. I told anyone who listened that I was not going to have the baby. I had decided against it. I was in active labor, but could not come to terms with what was happening.

Emily drove me to the hospital, and stayed for a few hours. She let me know that she was not interested in

witnessing me give birth, and I didn't blame her. My
boyfriend tried to come in the room several times, but I
didn't want him there. Finally I was so exhausted that I
relented and let him in. The sight of him made me feel
wronged. We both made this baby, so why was I the only
one having to go through the pain of having it?

He kept trying to tell me things like "relax" and
"breathe," and I just wished he would leave me alone. He
was trying to help, but I was scared and having a difficult
labor, and nothing he did could help that.

I was in active, but slow, labor. I stayed in the hospital
not one night, but two. The doctors wanted to send me
home, but because of my previous complications, they let
me stay.

I had one nurse who was able to calm and soothe me.
She came and talked to me about my fears, and told me that
my mind played a very powerful role in either making labor
easier or more difficult. She told me I had to relax and "let
the baby out" or they would be forced to do a C-section.
She dimmed all the lights and rubbed my back for me.

I was so exhausted by the second day that they gave me
a morphine drip so I could sleep. Finally after some rest, I
was ready to "let the baby out." I got an epidural, and very
calmly tried to tell myself that this was natural, and that
soon I would get to meet my baby.

I listened to the nurses and focused on one goal, trying to
see my baby. I hadn't confirmed the sex of the baby, but
was still convinced from my dream that I was having a
baby girl. I decided that if it was a girl, I was going to name
her Faith.

After I pushed out the baby's head and one arm, the

doctor told me that he was 95 percent sure that there were girl fingers on the baby's hand.

I got excited for the first time during my labor. I gasped, "I knew it was a girl, I dreamed about her!" And then, with one final push, I stopped being a pregnant girl and became a mother.

I didn't expect to feel the way I did when my child was born. I felt kind of detached and I was exhausted. I felt like I didn't have enough time to adjust to the fact that my baby was really here. I held her and asked the nurse to take my camera and take our picture, and then it seemed like chaos broke loose in the room. Faith's father, my family, and my friends all descended on the room, cheerful and energetic.

But I didn't want visitors. I just wanted chocolate milk. I hadn't eaten in two days, and my body was shaking uncontrollably. The last thing I remember was being in the delivery room drinking two cartons of chocolate milk, then waking up a day later in a strange room with a nurse telling me I had to get up to go to the bathroom.

It took me a few minutes to realize where I was. I started calling out for my baby. Another girl was behind a curtain that divided the room. She looked like she was twelve or thirteen, and I later found out that she was fifteen.

She popped her head out and said, "Girl or boy?"

"Girl," I told her.

"I had a boy," she said. "Maybe our kids will be in school together one day."

"Yeah, probably so," I told her, smiling.

A nurse brought Faith in, and I got to enjoy her for the

first time. She was so cute and little that I couldn't believe
she was mine. I held her and looked at her for a long time.
Then the nurse told me that it was her feeding time and
asked me if I wanted to breastfeed.

I didn't want to breastfeed at first because I thought it
seemed too weird. Only after the hospital sent in a woman
from La Leche League, and I found out how much I would
have to pay for formula did I change my mind. She also
told me how much better breastfeeding would be for Faith.

I learned how to nurse the baby in the hospital. It was a
good decision, and after a day or two, it didn't feel strange.
It felt natural, and how convenient not to wash bottles and
prepare formula!

My parents came to pick me up at the hospital and take
me back to my apartment. Faith's dad had to work, and I
was all alone with the baby. I tried to lay her down in her
crib and she screamed. I tried to hold her and she screamed.
Nothing I did seemed to pacify her.

I was terrified, and I knew that the hospital made a huge
mistake letting me walk out with a baby. What were they
thinking? I had no idea what I was doing!

I started to cry right along with the baby. I was sore from
my episiotomy (small cut to enlarge the vaginal opening),
and I was tired. I laid the baby down beside me in the bed
and started to nurse her. She calmed down and fell asleep,
and I put her in her cradle. I went to sleep just to wake up
in what seemed like minutes later. The baby was screaming
again, this time with thick green gunk dripping out of the
sides of her diaper.

I just sat there and stared at her and felt detached from
her. She was red from crying, she smelled bad, and I stared

at her and wanted her to shut up. I didn't want to change her smelly, gross diaper, and I didn't want to keep getting awakened by a crying baby. I was tired and cranky, and I wanted someone else to help me. I got on the phone to call Emily, but she wasn't home. I tried a couple of other friends who told me they couldn't hear me with the baby crying beside me.

Finally, after I couldn't take the screaming anymore, I grabbed a pillow and felt the urge to put it over the baby to make her stop screaming. The thought scared me so badly that I called my mother and told her that I couldn't get Faith to stop screaming.

My mother rarely came over to my apartment, but that day she came over quickly. She took Faith out of her crib and told me that she had a fever. She asked me if I had baby medicine, and I told her I had Infant Tylenol™. She showed me how to give it to her with the little dropper, and then she took a cool rag and began to wipe the baby with it. Slowly Faith stopped screaming and I began to feel normal again. I felt so horrible for wanting to put a pillow over my baby. I was sure I was a bad mother already.

My mother stayed so I could take a nap, and when I woke up, I felt a little better. I remembered reading about postpartum depression and the "baby blues," and I wondered if maybe I had it. Faith woke up again, and I changed her diaper and nursed her until she fell asleep. It was the first time I actually understood what it was like to feel like a mother. I remember staring at her and realizing that she was mine. It was scary, exciting, and wonderful, all at the same time.

The next day I made an appointment to see the doctor. I

told him that I felt moody, like I was going to do things to hurt the baby. He talked to me about stress, fatigue, and hormonal changes that might cause this. He told me that we should keep an eye on it to see if things got better if I slept more. I began to nap whenever Faith did. I told my employer that I wasn't coming back right away like I planned so I could recover from my pregnancy. Faith's dad began to give me more money to pay the bills, and as I got caught up on my sleep, I began to feel better.

As I felt better, I learned to enjoy the baby more. I loved holding Faith and watching her tiny fingers and toes wiggle. Her father and I didn't have much to talk about, but we always agreed that we thought she was the cutest thing we ever saw.

Life began to take on a new kind of normal, and I learned each day how hard, yet rewarding, it was to be a parent.

"Safe Haven" Can Help Avoid Tragedy

During my first year in college, twin newborns were found on campus in a trash can. They were dead, and their mother was never identified.

Tragically, a baby is left to die at least every other day in the United States. Approximately 250 cases of newborn babies killed or left for dead are reported to the Department of Justice each year. It is impossible to know the real number. In a few cases, an abandoned newborn is discovered in time and given a second chance at life.

Society often believes that a pregnant girl must give up her own life in order to have an unplanned child. Families, teachers, and friends often send an unmistakable message to a young single mother that an unplanned pregnancy is a tragedy. The fear of living this tragedy is the basis for the hopelessness many pregnant girls are experiencing. They live in fear and shame, and do not know where to turn.

Having a child is not a tragedy, although often the circumstances surrounding the pregnancy may be. A girl who has been raped, is substance abusing, or is not capable of handling a baby, should be allowed to leave a baby, anonymously, at a safe location.

*Safe Haven laws allow mothers to leave unwanted children in safe locations, with no questions asked. These laws are now on the books in most states. Hospitals, police stations, and fire houses are most often designated as safe locations. If you have hidden your pregnancy or know someone who has, and you don't know what to do now, **call someone** to find out where you can safely leave your baby. If you call **1-877-796-HOPE**, someone there will help you.*

Did You Know . . .

Postpartum depression is a real medical problem?

I briefly mention my postpartum problems in this chapter, but I could probably write an entire book about the strange behavior that haunted me for almost a year after the birth of my child. Diet, sleep, and the fact that I walked regularly helped me. But I know now that I may have needed medication that I didn't get. Anyone who experiences serious symptoms of depression or lack of sleep needs to speak up and seek help! Too often, doctors and family do not take these issues seriously. However, big emotional changes from hormonal factors are a real medical illness that must be treated.

It is important to realize that *depression is a physical disorder*, and is not just a bad mood. The person may not appear to be "depressed." She may seem panicked, worried all the time, or feel stress symptoms such as chest or neck pain and headaches. The bottom line is, when you notice that you *don't feel normal*, it is time to see a doctor to be sure that everything is okay.

Mood disorders during pregnancy and after childbirth are caused primarily by hormonal changes that then affect the brain. Very young moms may suffer these illnesses more than older women, not only because of their fragile hormonal balance, but also because stress from lack of partner support, financial worries, and social isolation negatively affect one's mental state. These moms need the most emotional, social, and physical support during pregnancy and after the birth, but are the least likely to get it.

The U.S. Department of Health and Human Services advises that you seek help from a doctor IMMEDIATELY for the following depression symptoms (if they last longer than two weeks):

1. Feeling restless or irritable, sad, hopeless, or overwhelmed.

2. Crying a lot or having no energy or motivation.

3. Eating and/or sleeping too little or too much.

4. Having trouble focusing, remembering, or making decisions.

5. Feeling worthless and guilty, or having a loss of interest or pleasure in activities.

6. Withdrawing from friends and family.

7. Having headaches, chest pains, heart palpitations, or hyperventilation.

8. After pregnancy, fear of hurting the baby or oneself, or not having interest in the baby.

4

Relationship + Problems = A Big Mess

*T*he pressure to get married, from family, society, and friends, seemed to start almost immediately when I found out I was pregnant, and got more frequent after Faith was born. I heard time and time again, "Oh, she's so cute! So, are you and her dad going to get married?"

My boyfriend seemed to love being a daddy during the first few months. He fussed and cooed over her. Even though our relationship was rocky, and we didn't see eye-to-eye on our future together, we decided to get married. It was a small ceremony.

Emily was maid-of-honor, but she wasn't thrilled by my impending nuptials. As she and I adjusted our dresses in the bathroom before the ceremony, she told me to give the word and she'd run outside, pull her car up, and we could escape before anyone noticed. She told me, "You and Faith will be in Canada before anyone knows what happened!"

I wish I had taken her up on her offer. By the time
Faith's dad and I pulled up to the local motel where we
were going to spend our "honeymoon" night, I knew I had
made a big mistake.

I broke down in tears as I walked into the motel bathroom and a roach ran across the floor. I was in a wedding
dress that began to stretch across my chest as my milk
came in for Faith's normal feeding time. My parents were
keeping her overnight, so I became engorged and milk
streamed down the front of me.

My new husband wanted what every groom expects on
his wedding night, but I didn't move from my spot on the
end of the bed where I sat crying. He started yelling at me
that this was what I wanted, to be married. Now I had better
put out. I hadn't been intimate with him during my uncomfortable months of pregnancy, and with Faith only being a
couple of months old, we hadn't done anything after she
was born either.

I told him "No," and sat there crying and leaking milk. I
told him I wasn't going to touch him, and that all of this
was his fault, and that I didn't want to be married. He
screamed and yelled and kicked the bed, and eventually fell
asleep. I sat up until morning in my soggy wedding dress.
Only then did I shower and change, so I could hurry back
to my baby so she could nurse.

I didn't tell anyone what happened. I just went home
and privately tried to figure out how to get out of the
mess I was in. I kept thinking, "Why did I get married? I
was allowed to start dating only a year ago. This isn't love.
I want a happy, forever marriage, and this isn't it!"

Eventually I told my mother that I had made a mistake,

and that I didn't want to be married. My mother told me that marriage is hard when you are in love with someone, but it is impossible if you are not in love. She asked me if I had felt pressure to get married because of her and my father's expectations. I told her yes, because I wanted them to be proud of me. I knew that being an unmarried mom wouldn't make them proud.

She told me that I was not a child anymore, and that I needed to figure out what I was going to do next. I went home and told Faith's dad that we made a mistake. He just yelled at me and called me every bad name he could think of. He said, "My parents got divorced, and I had to go through a lot of bad stuff because of it. We are *not* getting divorced."

I argued with him that what we were doing wasn't a "real marriage," but in the end he told me he wasn't going to give me a divorce. Instead, he just moved out and ignored the divorce paperwork that I sent him from the free Legal Aid clinic. He began to get more heavily involved with his party scene, and I got more and more into being a mommy. Eventually he stopped coming around at all. I called and begged him to stay a part of Faith's life. I wrote him letters asking him to go to court and get a visitation schedule. But, after a while, I had no idea where he was. Faith noticed his disappearance, but was not distressed since, after the first year, he was so rarely there anyway.

I made my life so much more complicated than it had to be. Now I had to jump through hurdles to get a divorce without his cooperation. By the time I got one, he hadn't called or come by to see Faith in over a year. I was angry and bitter, and didn't even want his name mentioned to me.

I became Mom *and* Dad. It was stressful, frustrating, and

as Faith began to understand more things, I felt bad and guilty that she didn't know who her father was. She was hustled and bustled around on my schedule, and had to deal with my impatience and lack of time. I did the best I could to make life normal for her.

I tried to keep the same routine: Get up, shower, eat, take Faith to daycare, go to work, go back to pick Faith up, go home or to the library, play for a while, give Faith a bath, feed her, clean up my apartment, read, go to sleep, and start all over again. The routine kept me sane, and I felt I was accomplishing something.

Emily and I started to drift apart as our lives took separate paths. She was young, single, and wanted to travel and work in theater. I always had to think about when to be home and what hours I was working at my second job as a waitress.

My parents would sometimes watch Faith so I could have some free time to myself. I started dating, eventually becoming serious with a guy who was in college. I soaked up as much college life as I could through him. It felt good that someone with no kids, who was in college, actually chose me to date.

I thought that I was living the best life I could, for someone in my "situation." I figured that I was doing pretty good if I could pay the bills, take care of my kid alone, and still have some time for a boyfriend. For a long time, I didn't think that anything was wrong with my life. I didn't dare to dream anything bigger than what I had. No one told me that I should go to college, or anywhere else, for that matter. I never thought to leave my hometown with a child, or to go see anywhere other than my backyard.

But . . . somewhere inside me, an itch started. It started

out so small that I could only feel it in the quietest moments of the night. As the years droned on, it grew stronger and more persistent. Finally it was clawing inside of me, attacking me from the inside out, and screaming, "More! You can do more than this!"

Maybe you are feeling that itch, too. Maybe it's why you picked up this book. Maybe you know that you have more to offer life than you are currently giving it. Maybe there are no maybes. Perhaps there are only choices we make either to live life to the fullest, or choose just to exist.

If you never graduated from high school, or wanted to go to college, but didn't . . . if you have some other dream, but thought you couldn't fulfill it with a baby . . . I'm going to tell you what I eventually learned.

You can do it.

You can achieve any goal that you want, as long as you make a plan, follow through with it, and believe in yourself.

I know that some of you will have a ton of excuses for why you can't reach some of the goals or dreams you have for yourself. You're on welfare, you're not married, you didn't finish high school, you're not old enough to work or drive, you live with your parents, your parents kicked you out, you have more than one child, you did drugs, you need to work, you don't think you're a good mom, you've been arrested, or you have no friends left since the baby.

I said some of those things to myself. I felt doubt that I could accomplish anything while I was tired and stained from thrown-up baby food. Most of my non-parent friends abandoned me like I was a leper, and my single-parent friends helped me reinforce my self-doubt. It seemed they also believed it was impossible for them to follow dreams for their lives, and still be good mommies.

As the years went on I met more and more girls like me. These girls got pregnant and sat home dreaming of what their lives should have been like, but not really doing anything to change it. Some were single and had no help from the fathers, and some had fathers that were always there for their kids, but either way, most of them put their own lives on hold after becoming young mommies.

For years, I believed the statistics and hype that my circumstances meant I couldn't do all the things I wanted to do. Luckily, I graduated from high school before my child was born, but my dream was to go to college, to be a journalist or a teacher. I was content to let that dream slip away because of the belief that I couldn't survive college with a kid.

Before I decided I *really* wanted to change my circumstances, all of the obstacles in my life seemed too large to get over. After I made the decision to change my life, I was surprised at the creative ways I found to achieve my objectives. The funny part is, it can be simple to follow a plan that will allow you to achieve the things you want.

The hardest part will be convincing yourself that you are good enough, smart enough, and brave enough to live out your dreams. This may mean fighting an internal battle with yourself. You may feel depression or guilt associated with your past, your current situation, or a number of other life circumstances.

Don't let those feelings win. Make a plan to have a better, more exciting and fulfilling life. Don't live life always wondering *"What if . . ."*

Do You Know . . .

What self-esteem is?

*T*here is no shame in feeling bad about yourself, or your life, from time to time. But before you are a harder judge on yourself than you are on everyone else, just remember that there is not one person in this life who will get out *without having messed up something* in his or her life. Messing things up is just part of life and shouldn't make your self-esteem suffer!

If you have a problem feeling good about yourself, chances are you didn't give that problem to yourself. Low self-esteem comes from being around the wrong people, whether those people are your family, friends, or love interest. The wrong people tell you things that make you think that you are a screw-up or that you're not good enough. They criticize you, yell at you, or hit you. They neglect you, tease you, ignore you, or expect you to be perfect.

If this describes your relationship with someone you know, then you should realize that the feeling you get from them, the one that makes you feel like you are "not good enough," is a LIE!

No matter how many times you have screwed things up, no matter how many times you have disappointed people, you need to know one powerful thing: *Your future life is not a reflection of your past.* You can start over . . . in a new environment and around new people if you choose.

You can live whatever life you want to live *as long as you believe that you deserve it!*

5

Turning Points

*I*f you don't already know what you want from your life, try to figure it out! Take a piece of paper and begin writing down all the things that you DON'T like about your current situation. After you have that list, it will probably be easy to decide what things you want to change. It will be easy to write a "GOAL" list.

Your GOALS will be what you focus on when you are tired or weak, or struggling with life. They will be your focal point . . . your light at the end of the tunnel. Ultimately, they will be the things that change you and your child(ren)'s lives. You need to really want it, really believe it, and be willing to work hard to get it.

The day I started to write my GOALS on paper, it was an accident. It was January, and I lived in Pennsylvania. There was a blizzard outside, and we got almost three feet of snow. Since everything in town was shut down, I got an unexpected day off work.

Trapped and stir crazy, I was trying to keep warm in the tiny efficiency apartment my daughter and I lived in, when suddenly I started to cry. It was a blubbering, slobbery, full-out cry, and I didn't know where in the world it had come from!

I went into my bathroom so I wouldn't upset my daughter who was oblivious, laughing at something on the TV, and I composed myself. When I looked at myself in the bathroom mirror, I lost control and started to cry again.

I couldn't grasp what was happening, so I did what I had always done when I was upset: I started to write. With all the sobbing I was doing, it was as if my pen was writing without any help from me. I found myself making a list of things I had been upset about. It read:

1. My boyfriend is a jerk.

2. I hate my jobs.

3. I don't have a car.

4. I am poor.

5. I hate this crappy town.

6. I saw a roach in the hall.

7. I want to go to college.

8. I'm starting to think Ramen noodles are good.

9. I'm always tired.

10. Faith and I need new clothes.

11. We try to keep warm with the popcorn popper.

I felt a little better after venting to myself, so after a while I put my list down, bathed my daughter, and put her to bed. Later, I picked up my list and one thing stood out to me over the rest — Number 7: *I want to go to college.*

Now, I had said those words in the past. I had told

everyone that I would do it "one day." But I had *never written it down before*. I had never really thought about how to do it.

But my list got me thinking about college . . . a lot. I thought about it as I showered for bed, I thought about it as I ironed my uniform for my job at a restaurant, and I thought about it as I stood in piles of snow waiting for the bus the next morning.

I remembered getting an acceptance letter to college and reading the letter over my giant pregnant belly, with tears in my eyes. I told myself that day, "Well, there will be no going to college now," and tore the letter up in disgust.

Now I thought differently about it. I thought about it so much that after work the following day, I looked for the list I had written. I drew a big circle around *I want to go to college*, folded the paper, and put it in my wallet as a reminder to myself.

I took out a new piece of paper and a pencil, and wrote on the top of the page, "THINGS I WILL DO WITH MY LIFE." Under the heading I wrote:

1. Graduate from college.

Then I stopped writing. I realized I didn't have a clue what I needed to do to go to college!

I thought about a friend of mine who was in college, and wondered how she was doing. I looked up her number in my address book, called her, and without making any small talk, asked her what she had done to get into college.

She told me that first she decided why she wanted to go to college. She wanted to be a nurse. She went to the guidance counselor at school and asked him about the best colleges for nursing. He requested catalogs for her and talked to her about her options. Finally, she and her parents reviewed the catalogs and talked about which college they could afford, how much financial aid she would need, and they all picked out a school together. *Then bluebirds flew in the window, landed on her shoulder, and whistled while she sang the college song from her new school,* I thought.

Frustrated, I put my list down. I wasn't in high school, didn't have a guidance counselor, had no idea where to get financial aid, and I had no money of my own. I was one bad payday away from a shelter, and I wasn't going to my parents for thousands of dollars for college.

I remembered seeing a brochure that had come in the mail that day from Penn State, so I picked it up and looked at the option for night school. The classes were expensive, but I thought I could probably afford one class each semester. At that rate, it would take me *20 years* to graduate from college! I thought that would be ridiculous so I folded up the paper with "THINGS I WILL DO WITH MY LIFE" written on it, and put it in my wallet with the other one.

That night, in an attempt to solidify my self-pity, I watched a news show about youth violence in America. The show talked about the number of violent offenders and victims of violent offenders that came from one-parent, poverty-level households. I went to sleep that night feeling depressed and upset. I was tired of my life being one long day after another. I was tired of struggling for money. But now I didn't think college was a possibility. I couldn't afford it, and didn't know where to get the help I needed. I put going to college out of my mind, and finally fell asleep.

Whatever your goal (and I realize it may not include college), you need to decide what *you need to do to achieve that goal.*

Did You Know . . .

When people are confused about what to do, they often do nothing?

*D*oing nothing is a choice that very seldom makes your life any better. Things happen for people who make them happen. Take control of your life, make a plan, and work hard. Your future begins now! What is your next step? Have you thought about what you're going to do with your life?

It may seem hard to believe, but you will grow old one day. When you do, you will either look back regretfully and say, "I wish I would have," or you will laugh and feel full, saying, "Remember when I did . . ." Your children will grow older, and you will not get a second chance to hug them, talk to them, and play with them. You will not have a second chance to make them believe that they can do whatever they set their mind to.

Living your dreams does not mean that you have to become a doctor, lawyer, or go to work in a suit every day. It means that you look inside yourself and find out what your secret wishes are for your future. Don't miss out on one minute of this potential adventure we call life! Travel, make friends, learn, see new things, read, teach your children, volunteer, spend your time helping others.

"The human race is filled with passion. Medicine, law, business, and engineering, these are noble pursuits and necessary to sustain life. But poetry, beauty, romance, love, these are what we stay alive for." Dead Poets Society, 1989. Enjoy your life. Do the things that you are passionate about. Dream, plan, and then live!

6

Never Write
Your Goals In Pencil

I don't remember what it was that made me fold up
those pieces of paper and put them in my wallet. I'm
glad I did. Several weeks later, on a trip to the public
library with my daughter, those papers changed my life.

I was sitting in the children's section when my daughter
asked me if I had something in my purse that she could
write on. I opened my purse and saw the two folded pages
sticking out of my wallet. I pulled one out and was about to
give it to her. Then she asked me if I had another one for
the friend she was playing with. I took out both papers and
handed them to her.

The girls started complaining that my papers had writing
on them. The other girl's mother walked over and sat down
with us. She and I had spoken a few times before while our
daughters met for story time.

"I think I have paper," she said, looking in her bag.

Her daughter said, "Mine has just a little writing on it, in pencil. Do you have an eraser, Mommy?"

The girl's mother saw the words on my paper and said, "Wait a minute, this is Faith's mommy's important paper."

Then she gave the girls two fresh sheets of paper from a notebook in her bag, and she handed me my papers.

"Don't you know you should never write your goals in pencil?" she asked. "If you do, you don't really see them as permanent."

I fumbled with my papers, folded them up, and mumbled something about them not really being goals.

She smiled at me and said, "I think you'd do great in college. Do you know where you want to go?"

I politely told her that I didn't have the money to go to college, and she laughed.

"Money!" she exclaimed. "You don't need money to go to college, you just need student loans!"

I then explained to her what the credit report of a broke, single mother looked like, and she said, "They don't base your student loans on your credit. Besides, there are all kinds of grants and scholarships that you would probably qualify for. You should go to the resource center downstairs and get some books about it."

What? Why hadn't anyone told me this before? I shouted inside my head. I don't remember anything she said to me after that. My mind was downstairs in the resource room of the library, thinking of the information I wanted to find.

I thanked her, then pulled Faith away from her friend so I could go downstairs. I asked the librarian where I could find information on student loans and grants. She led me to the right section, and I dove into those books like a starving man at a buffet dinner!

I put Faith on my lap so she could draw with her paper

and pencil as I read through the resource books I collected from the shelves. Although I didn't understand all the ins and outs of student loans in one day, I did learn enough at the library to know that not only could I get enough money for classes, but I could also get a little extra for living expenses. This meant I could quit one of my two jobs and replace it with school. Something that would help secure my future!

I also learned that what the other mother told me about not needing money for school is only partly true. It is true that your credit history doesn't matter for some types of student loans, but for others, it may. And, of course, the minute I was out of college and started paying back my loans, I realized it was *real* money.

The Stafford loan is what I eventually got. It is the most popular type of student loan. With a Stafford loan, the student is the borrower, so most people who take out Stafford loans have little or no credit history. That is one reason why, when you apply for one, the lender doesn't look at your credit report. That means that you could have no credit history at all, or your credit score could be horrible, and you could still qualify for a Stafford loan.

Another federally guaranteed student loan, the Perkins, is for the neediest of students. It's a good resource for single parents. With a Perkins loan, the school is the lender, but the federal government supplies the money. Credit history doesn't matter in applying for a Perkins loan either.

Before I left the library that day, I took the piece of paper with "THINGS I WILL DO WITH MY LIFE" written on it, and smoothed it out on the table. I thought about what the little girl's mother had said about not writing your goals in pencil, so I pulled a pen out of my purse and traced over the words I had written:

1. Graduate from college

I had written down that goal weeks earlier, but that day was the first time I *believed* that I could do it. It was the first dream of a long list of dreams that I eventually wrote on that paper. For the next few months, even though I still woke up, went to work, and repeated my old routine, my life had changed. *I started making plans for a better future.*

As I look back now, I realize I had no idea of the journey I was about to embark on. I also didn't know that for the next seven years, that piece of yellow legal paper would be with me across states and continents, until every one of the goals I had put on it that year had been crossed off.

You may never encounter someone who can tell you the right direction to head when trying to achieve your dreams. Instead, you may have to research and seek out information on your own. Information is powerful, and goes hand-in-hand with believing that you can achieve your goals. The saying, if there's a will, there's a way, means that sometimes you just have to keep looking for ways to achieve your goals.

In the same light, you can be anything you want to be, but you cannot do the impossible. You cannot set a goal to become rich overnight, and expect it to happen. You cannot usually set a goal to meet a gorgeous, wealthy, soul-mate, and take steps to accomplish it. The most common reason that will stop you from living a good, successful life is misjudging your ability to achieve your goal.

A plan can change your life if you let it. It is up to you to choose a goal that excites you and is achievable. You can decide that you want to be a hairdresser or an astronaut, a mechanic or an archeologist, but the process for achieving your goal will be the same:

1. Decide on your goal.

2. Figure out what steps you need to take to get there.

3. Make a plan.

4. Find the resources you need to achieve the plan.

5. Take action and *begin following your plan.*

Just like the directions on the back of a cake box, there will be things you need to do in order to have your recipe come out good. If you are baking a cake, first you need to figure out what ingredients you need. If you forget the egg, the cake won't turn out the way you expected.

The same way with your goals. You can't decide to be a doctor, but not want to go to college for years. So recognize reality and follow the recipe. It may take some time to get the recipe right, but if you have high standards and set challenging goals for yourself, you can be whatever you want to be!

My dream was to go to college because I loved learning, reading, and wanted to become a writer or a teacher. Your goals may be completely different than mine. You may think, "I don't want to go to college. I want to be a truck driver, or a musician, or a carpenter." But the fact of the matter is, no matter what your goal is, you need to make plans on how to achieve it.

If you don't plan for it, it will never happen. You will always be living in the moment, trying to survive day-to-day. But the moment you decide on wanting to do "something" is the day you have to decide if college or trade school, or on-the-job training is how you will achieve it.

The bottom line is, if you *do not believe* you can accomplish the goals you write down, you will ultimately give up and fail at them. *The desire to achieve your dreams* is the number one factor that will determine your success.

Just remember, you don't have to do a hundred tasks this week. You have a child and must not stretch yourself too thin or you will find yourself short-tempered and lashing out at your child. Instead, set manageable "To-Do" tasks that you can fit into your daily schedule. See Appendix, pp. 155-158, for a sample plan, and start developing *your* goals and strategies for meeting those goals.

Don't forget that you are striving to make your total quality of life better, so your daily tasks can include things like exercise, prayer, meditation, healthy eating, and spending quality time with your children. These things will help you feel better, be more motivated, and be better able to manage your stress.

Do You Know . . .

How to start setting goals for yourself?

The biggest difference between a career without college and one that requires it is the money you make. Over time, however, if you gain skills and have job stability, you can make a reasonable salary without a college degree.

So before you start writing your goals, make sure they are realistic. *This doesn't mean that you can't be a lawyer or even an astronaut if you want to . . . it means that you should realistically size up your abilities.* If you really hate school, it may not be realistic to aim for a career that requires a college degree with a lot of academics. An apprentice program or vocational school may be a better route for you.

- Take the time to really think about what you would like to do with your life.

- Write those ideas down, and pick the ones you would like to make your reality.

- List the things you think you will have to do to reach those dreams.

Be Sure To:

☐ Do something to work toward your goal EVERY SINGLE DAY!

☐ Find every resource you can (i.e. free vocal lessons at school or financial aid for cosmetology school).

☐ Research, study, and learn everything you can about your dreams and goals.

☐   As you learn more, add tasks to your list of things you need to do to achieve your goal.

☐   Do not give up or procrastinate, or you will not progress.

For example, if your dream is to become a professional singer or a hairstylist, you must set short-term goals that will help you accomplish the dream:

Goal: To become a professional singer

1. *Set aside one hour per day to practice singing.*
2. *Get a set (list of songs) that I will learn and perfect for a show.*
3. *Research contests and competitions that I can use to get experience and exposure.*
4. *Save up small amounts of money each week or each month to get a demo CD made.*
5. *Begin sending out demo CDs to clubs and asking if I can audition for them.*

Goal: To become a hairstylist

1. *Complete grade 12 or get a GED to enter cosmetology school.*
2. *Look in the phone book for a hairstyling trainee program and call for information.*
3. *Buy hair and fashion magazines and videos to keep up with fashion trends in hairstyles.*
4. *Practice visualizing how hairstyles will work with people's physical features.*
5. *Practice on all nationalities and types of hair.*
6. *Offer to practice on friends and family while you're in training.*

Solving Reading Problems

There are 25 million adults in the United States who can not read. These adults read very little or not at all because they were not taught as children. They did not have an adult in their life that sat with them every night and helped them read, or they had a learning disability that was not diagnosed and treated.

The statistics about literacy are frightening. Three out of four children in the U.S. do not have the skills to write stories or reports for school. More than 20 percent of adults read at or below a fifth grade level. 70 percent of people who read below a sixth grade level have no full or part-time job. Not being able to read well can be a big stumbling block as you work toward a better future for yourself and your child.

If you have not graduated from high school, or you're having trouble in school, an alternative school where you can be noticed and encouraged can help you improve your reading skills and earn a high school diploma.

Talk to your school counselor about the possibility of getting a tutor (at no charge to you) to help you learn to read better. Also, ask your teacher or librarian to suggest books that you might like to read. Check out books to read to your child. The more you read, the more your reading skills will improve. So keep reading!

Too many pregnant girls don't get their education, and they end up with low-skill, low-paying jobs that offer no future. Sometimes the key to a better future lies in improving your reading ability.

Take control of your education. Insist on getting help if you need it.

7

What's Your Money Plan?

Money will probably be your number one worry as a young parent. I found there was only one way for me as a struggling mom to get control of my money. It is a formula I call "Daily Living," and it is very simple:

1. Figure out the amount of money you will definitely take home for the month.

2. Deduct the money you will spend for essential bills (rent, gas, electric) from that amount.

3. The money you have left over after paying these bills is your "Daily Living" money.

4. Divide this total amount of "Daily Living" money by the number of days in the month.

5. The number you get is the daily amount of money that you have to spend on everything you need (food, diapers, hygiene products, and other necessities).

Example of "Daily Living"

I got paid $400 every two weeks. This meant that for a month I took home around $800.

My rent took the bulk of my pay at $525 per month. I deducted my rent ($525) from my income ($800) and realized that I had only $275 per month left to eat, have transportation, buy hygiene products, diapers and wipes, and pay my other bills.

I had no car and no cable, only basic telephone and electric of $60 per month. I took my figure of $275 and deducted $60 from it. That left me with $215 per month for "Daily Living" (bus, food, hygiene, and baby care items).

I divided my $215 by the number of days in the month. Dividing $215 by 30 (days in a month) would leave me with $7.16 to spend each day. It seemed like I had more to work with if I said, "I have $7.00 to spend every single day."

That $7.16 would be my money for each day. However, if I didn't spend all of my $7.16 in one day, the leftover amount would carry over into the next day. For example:

Monday: Spent $2.50 on the bus, bought 80 pack of baby wipes for $1.99.
- Total for day = $7.16
- Total spent = $4.49
- Amount left = $2.67 (carry over to Tuesday)

Tuesday: Spent $2.50 on the bus.
- Total for day = $7.16 + $2.67 = $9.83
- Total spent = $2.50
- Amount left = $7.33 (carry over to Wednesday)

Wednesday: Spent $2.50 on the bus, bought diapers on sale for $5.99.

- Total for day = $7.16 + $7.33 = $14.49
- Total spent = $8.49
- Amount left = $6.00 (carry over to Thursday)

Thursday: Spent $2.50 on the bus.
- Total for day = 7.16 + 6.00 = $13.16
- Total spent = $2.50
- Amount left = $10.66 (carry over to weekend)

Friday, Saturday, Sunday: 99 cents store and groceries: $31.90.
- Total for the weekend ($7.16 x 3 days + $10.66 carried over from Thursday) = $32.14
- Total spent: $31.90
- Amount left: $0.24

This formula is a valuable tool for managing your money each month. I made it a personal challenge to find discount grocery stores and cool thrift stores where I could buy items inexpensively. I waited until the weekend to do my grocery shopping for the week. That way I used all the money that carried over through the week on my food and hygiene products. I went to discount grocery stores, clipped coupons, and ate a lot of pasta, rice, and noodles. I also looked for programs like WIC (Special Supplemental Feeding Program for Women, Infants, and Children) that could provide me with some additional food.

Whether you are single or not, if you find that you do not make enough money to pay all of your bills and buy necessities with a "Daily Living" plan, then you probably need to rethink your expenses or living arrangements. Turn off the cable, get rid of your car and ride the bus, get a roommate, live temporarily with your parents, or move to a smaller, less expensive apartment. It will be a temporary way to gain control of your money while you go to school or get training for a career that will pay you more money.

I knew nothing about credit reports, money, or budgeting until after my credit was already ruined. No one ever taught me how to manage my money. I didn't know how valuable good credit was. A poor credit score makes it hard to get a credit card. This means you will pay higher interest rates on loans. It means you may be turned down for a job, and you may not be able to rent a house or an apartment. It is embarrassing, and makes people see you as irresponsible.

Money becomes much less of a worry if you have a plan for it. Reckless spending and not understanding your money is dangerous and has left many people either homeless, or on the verge of being homeless. Making a budget is one of the first things to do if you're trying to change your life.

I still use a daily living plan, even though now I also have a financial planner who understands more complicated investments, and I have a savings plan. I live modestly and do not splurge on a lot of "stuff." I know that "stuff" like fancy cars, boats, clothes, and jewelry doesn't mean that I will never be poor again. Those items just go down in value over the years, while the money I save (by not buying those things) gains interest and goes up in value.

Most young mothers do not save any money because they often don't have enough to cover basic expenses. However, a savings account with a couple hundred dollars in it could save you in the event of an emergency. Single parents, more than any other population, need the backup of a savings account. I know it seems impossible, but you can open a savings account with as little as five dollars, and then commit to adding a dollar or two each week. You will be surprised to see how quickly your money grows.

Keisha Made Money
While Working in Her Living Room

*I*t all started when I went to a flea market with my
grandmother. She was picking up odds and ends at
different tables when I saw a stand that had homemade
baby blankets and clothing.

I walked to the stand to look at the price tags on the
clothes and blankets. They were nice, but I couldn't believe
they were selling those tiny outfits for over ten dollars
each! Their blankets ran between fifteen and twenty-five
dollars, although I knew it probably only cost them a dollar
or two for the kind of fabric they used.

There were a bunch of people looking at and buying the
clothes, and I thought to myself, "I can do this! I can make
extra money making and selling baby clothes and blan-
kets." When I was pregnant, I handmade dozens of pretty
things for my daughter, Kayli. My grandmother raised me,
and she was good at sewing, knitting, and crocheting. She
taught me how to do all three when I was really young.

I told my grandmother about my idea, and she was so
excited, she went right over to the management to find out
how we could set up a table each week. It was only ten
dollars a week.

I worked at KFC during the day, and every night I sewed
after Kayli went to bed. I bought the fabric and yarn to use
for dresses and bonnets while my grandmother knitted the
baby blankets.

After two months, we had about 40 items made. I de-
cided to sell the items for slightly less than the items I saw
at the first flea market stand. To make my items more

attractive, I added a free gift to every purchase (a rattle from the discount store). I tied the product and the gift together with a pink, blue, or yellow ribbon.

The first day at the flea market was a blur. I sold 27 items and left with over $340! That was almost $100 more than I earned in a week at KFC. I couldn't believe it. I had spent less than $30 on fabric, $10 on the flea market space, and made $300 profit.

For the next few months, I worked harder and faster to make products. My grandmother began looking for other swap meets, school or church yard sales, and flea markets where I could sell my items. I used the Internet as well, creating my own free website and selling on the Internet on free sites like Craigslist.

I found myself earning $200 to $400 each week, but I didn't quit my job at KFC. Instead, I started a savings account. Life is easier for me and Kayli with the extra money, but the best part is that I can work my "second job" during the hours that are good for me.

I suggest to any young mom to use her skills. I know that people are addicted to flea markets, so if you have a craft that you're good at, try selling items there or on the Internet. People look for my stand at the flea market now, and I even made business cards to hand out.

I am now looking into getting a business permit and a business checking account so I can sell at other types of functions as a vendor.

Sometimes, when I'm out, I see a baby wearing one of the outfits I made and I am proud of myself. I want to go to fashion design school now, and am looking into my options.

Did You Know . . .

Even single parents can save money?

Many people claim they don't have enough money to save anything after they have paid their bills. But this is not the case. If you have been to McDonalds, bought a soda, or went to the movies in any given month, you have just spent your savings.

Saving money takes discipline and a good understanding of why you are saving. If, starting in January, you put just $10 per week in a savings account that you don't touch, by the following Christmas you will have saved more than $500. By the end of five years, you will have $2,600, and that doesn't include the interest you will have earned by having money in the bank.

If you make a habit of saving this $10 each week, by the time your child is graduating from high school, you'll have almost $10,000 in the bank that can help put your "baby" through college.

Many of us spend $10 each week on unnecessary items like soda, coffee, fast food, movies, cigarettes, and candy. Take a good look at every dollar you spend. Where is your money going? Where can you find a few extra dollars to put in a savings account?

If you find that you are so swamped that you can't manage to save any money, then you need to come up with a new plan for your current situation. Move to a less expensive city or neighborhood. See what help you can get from social services, your community center, or your church for training, childcare, or job skills.

Do something to make your financial life better . . . control your money so it doesn't control you!

8

Some of Us Make Mistakes in Love

Managing money, as tough as it seems, is easy when I compare it to understanding men.

You notice that the number one complaint on the "Reasons I Am Sad" list was that my boyfriend was a jerk. But the crazy part is, it took me several years to realize that he was a jerk — and he wasn't even hiding it! He was good-looking and smart, and he was in college. I felt lucky that he picked me of all people to date. He wasn't my child's father, and showed very little interest in being a part of her life at all. Though I didn't realize it then, it was probably a good thing.

When I look back now, I get so upset at myself. He was egotistical and tried to belittle me for being a single mother. He told me many times that most guys wouldn't be able to put up with *a girl with a kid*. He was in college on his parent's dime, and worked part-time to be able to afford designer clothes and beer.

He never praised me for working two jobs and raising my child alone. He never told me what steps I could take to get into college. He played emotional games, and he never seemed to make my life easier. Still, somehow I was convinced that I needed him.

If you are a teen mom, you are most likely involved with a guy that is older than you. In 2002, nearly forty percent of teen mothers got pregnant by men aged 20 or older. What most starry-eyed teen girls don't realize is that only a tiny percentage of these adult men will ever marry the teen mothers of their children. Most of these relationships, whether the father is an older man or a teenager, will eventually break down, which means that teen mothers will have to enter the dating world with a child and a whole new set of issues.

Whether you are in a relationship or single, it is smart to make a good plan for your future, a future that can happen *with or without* a man in your life. This plan may be more valuable to you than any other resource you have. So, even though it may seem unromantic, planning for a future that *may not* include the person you are romantically involved with may be necessary. Have a "Plan B," and know you can go on with or without that person.

I certainly am not down on love. I think relationships can be wonderful and often make you feel good and optimistic. I had a mix of boyfriends while I was a single mother. I had wonderful times and thousands of laughs. I also had my heart broken and suffered through my fair share of tragedy. But whether my relationships were wonderful or not, most of the men I dated were just boyfriends, not *husbands* or *daddies*.

Faith's father was no help to me after the first year. I

never got any child support. He didn't call, write, or do
anything at all as her father. It would have been easy to get
caught up in how unfair that was, but I had better things to
do than spend my time trying to *make* him do right.

Yes, I was desperately poor. Yes, I felt used. Yes, I felt it
was unfair, but something inside me said, "Don't waste
your time trying to force someone else to be responsible."
Instead, I became responsible on my own. I certainly
wasn't perfect at it, but I worked hard to try to be a good
mom, and still be a normal young person who had a life.

I knew that my daughter wanted and needed a father. As
much as I tried to tell myself that she was fine and that the
situation was fine, she wanted and needed to hear about and
know who her *real* father was. I did my best to explain
things to her without putting my biased spin on the situation. I knew that her father might have been a good father if
he had been older and sober.

I made the mistake of telling my daughter that she could
look up to my boyfriends as "dads." As a single parent,
you may not even realize that you may be too quick to try
to make (and fake) a "family" with someone who is not
meant to be your life partner. It is a strong temptation to try
to fill the gap, but chances are you don't truly know yet
what love is supposed to look and feel like.

I know now that I confused love with other things along
the way. As a result, I have learned several things: Love is
not the rush of emotions and hormones that make you feel
dizzy and passionate. Love is *not* a desperate feeling to
keep someone. Love is *not* the hope that someone will love
you enough to stay.

The scariest part of dating for a single mom is her
children. Every time you break up with a boyfriend who

has gotten involved in your child's life, you may be bringing your child through their equivalent of a divorce.

My advice on men is to keep them separate from your children for as long as you can, until you are in a *very* committed relationship. This usually takes many months or years to accomplish.

I now realize that my child dated right along with me. When I broke up, she broke up. When I thought this would be "the one," she thought it also. It wasn't until she was around eight or nine that I realized that I had been bringing her along on my relationship highs and lows.

On one of my frequent library trips, I read that the chance of a single mother getting pregnant a second time before she is married is very high. For the youngest mothers the number is the highest. Twenty-five percent of teenage mothers have a second child within two years of their first, often by a different father.

I have seen it happen to my friends. Know that although you can still realize your dreams if you have more than one child, the more children you have, the longer and harder it will be for you to reach the goals you set. A young mother is more likely to reach her goals if she either abstains from sex or uses birth control every time she has intercourse.

I know that I have made relationship choices when I have been feeling insecure, lonely, or frustrated. I didn't feel as attractive as a girl without children, and I was jealous of my childless friends' lives. I just wanted someone to love me, and sometimes, without realizing it, I looked to a guy, thinking he could fill the emptiness I was feeling.

Many girls get pregnant a second time out of desperation, carelessness, or the mistaken belief that the guy will stay if she has his children. Even if she doesn't get pregnant again, if and when the boyfriend leaves her, she winds up confused, depressed, and blaming herself or her children for the breakup.

You could be left in an even worse situation by getting pregnant a second time. You may feel so overwhelmed that you can't reflect on what things you need to do to make things better. If you are living in crisis mode, constantly putting out immediate fires, your larger goals will be lost in the shuffle.

To find the right partner, you may have to put your love life on hold for a while. Then you can work on making yourself someone who can be an equal partner in your relationship.

*A*fter starting my list, I began to feel some independence from my boyfriend. I began to realize that I didn't really *need* him to have a good future. Somehow, I had believed that down the line we would get married, and that I would be a perfect wife, have more kids, and be satisfied.

But, after writing down my first dream, I started thinking of all kinds of things that I wanted to do with my life, and none of those things included him. I started to think about life after college, when I had a good job, and could afford daycare, vacations, and maybe a house. I started thinking about how nice it would be to live the new life I was going to create for myself. I started to become independent, and it felt great.

Jane — Abuse in a Relationship

Jane was my neighbor in the small apartment building where I lived when my daughter was a toddler. She had her first child at 15 and was emancipated from her mother shortly afterward. She got pregnant again a few years later while she was living in my building.

Her boyfriend was funny and good-looking. At least, that's what I saw during the day. One night, after Jane told me she was pregnant again, I heard screaming coming from her apartment. I ran into the hallway, and when I reached her door I couldn't believe it when I heard the things her boyfriend was saying to her.

"You stupid b*#$%, you and your daughter! Both stupid b*#$%s."

Then I heard her daughter, who was only three, start shrieking, "Get off my mommy! Mommy!"

I heard a loud crash, then Jane sobbing to her daughter, "Ali, go in the bathroom and lock the door! Now!"

I ran downstairs and called 911. I told them what was happening and what the emergency was. They wanted my name, and I told them that I wanted to be anonymous. Scared, I hung up.

A few minutes later the police knocked on my door. I guess they knew the call had come from my address. They asked me where the disturbance was, and I told them the number of Jane's apartment. I pressed my ear against the crack in my door to hear what happened next.

Jane answered the door, and the police asked her if there was a problem. I couldn't believe it when she told them, "No!"

The officers persisted, telling her that if she were in trouble, they could help her. They asked her boyfriend if there had been any trouble, and he said, "We were arguing, and she yells at me too loud." Then he laughed.

When the officers came back downstairs to leave, I met them on the front porch where Jane and her boyfriend couldn't see me.

"He was beating her! She's got a little girl in there and she's pregnant! Can't you do anything?"

The officers told me that they could only arrest him if she admitted something happened. They said they saw it every day, women who protected and stayed with the men who beat them.

Jane suffered all through her pregnancy. I heard the beatings, but never called the police again. She avoided me and all of the other neighbors after that night. She only made friendly small talk on her way in or out of her apartment.

Late one night I heard Jane in the hallway trying to waddle down the stairs. She was having her baby, and she was alone with her daughter. Her boyfriend had started staying out nights, and she needed a ride to the hospital. She had marks all over her arms and looked like she had been grabbed and squeezed until she bruised.

I tried to make her comfortable as I called a cab and rode with her and the kids to the hospital. She started to cry, looked at me and, very quietly, said, "I'm having a boy, his son. I need some help."

I told her to let them know at the hospital what she had been going through. I figured they could probably help her. I didn't know what else to tell her, so I just rubbed her back because I knew she was in pain, and I told her that everything was going to be okay.

The next morning her boyfriend came home after his night out, and I heard him knock on my door. I grabbed Faith and went into my bedroom and didn't answer the door. He went to another neighbor's door, and I heard him ask her if she had seen Jane. The lady told him, "No," and he left, cussing to himself.

Jane and her daughter never came back to her apartment again and I lost touch with her. The last time I saw her boyfriend was less than a month later when I saw him and a friend moving things out of the apartment. I always wondered how Jane was doing after having her baby.

I didn't find out until almost seven years later, in the parking lot of a bank. I had just flown in from Paris to visit my parents, and was surprised when Jane walked over to me, fit and happy. She gave me a bubbly, "Hi, Laura! How have you been?"

Her former three-year-old was now a tall, pretty, ten-year-old, and Jane had another child with her, a girl that looked too young to be the child she had seven years earlier.

I hugged her and asked her how she was and where her son was. She got very quiet as she said, "I released him for adoption the night you took me to the hospital. I went to a safe house after I got out of the hospital, and got my high school diploma and some secretarial training.

"I started working with the county government. I've been with them for almost six years now, and I just bought a house!"

She touched the little girl on the head, "This is Maile. I married her dad five years ago. She's four."

I was at a loss for what to say. I knew that she had wanted the son she was pregnant with all those years ago. I couldn't believe I never went to the hospital to see how she was, or to help her in any way. I was sure she must have thought I was an awful person, a terrible, so-called friend.

I just said, "I'm sorry you had to go through all that, but I'm glad you're happy now."

She opened her wallet and pulled out a picture of a handsome little boy that looked just like her ex-boyfriend.

"This is Tony," she said. "I have an open adoption, and I get pictures and letters from his family. I get to meet him in eleven more years when he's 18, unless his parents decide he can meet me sooner."

Little Maile pointed at the picture and said, "That's my brother, but he doesn't live with me,"

Jane put her kids in the car and pulled me aside. "I want to thank you for helping me that night. I've always thought about that. I had no money and no car — he made sure I was trapped there without him.

"I was going to walk to the hospital that night, because I knew that I was thinking about releasing the baby for adoption, and I didn't want him there. He attacked me the night I went into labor, before he left to go to his other girlfriend's house.

"The hospital took pictures of me and called the police. He never came to see me when I was in the hospital. Later, after I had placed the baby for adoption, I filed charges on him. He hardly got any jail time, but by the time he came looking for me, I was already dating Maile's dad.

"If you hadn't helped me, I would probably have ended up calling him for help, and I'd still be with him. I just couldn't raise that baby with a dad like that. You don't know how much your words meant to me."

My mouth hung open. I nodded, and told Jane I was happy for her. Then I excused myself and sat in my car in shock. I couldn't believe all that she had been through. I felt horrible for her thanking me, when I felt I hadn't done anything for her. I should have kept calling the police every time I heard him attacking her. I can't believe I just sat there and turned up my TV when it happened.

I was glad that she seemed happy, though I hoped, for her sake, that she would be able to spend time with her son before he was eighteen. I hope he will understand why she gave him up. She loved him enough to give him a better life.

Do You Know . . .

How to leave an abusive situation?

*T*he National Domestic Violence Hotline number is 1-800-799-SAFE. If you ever find yourself in this situation, and don't know where else to turn, call them and they can give you options. If you don't feel safe in your home, and you recognize some of the following things as familiar in your life, you may be a victim of domestic violence.

Does your boyfriend, partner, mother, father, or other family member do these things?

1. Constantly criticize you and your abilities as a person or parent?
2. Threaten to hurt you, your children, pets, family members, friends or him/herself?
3. Get angry or lose his/her temper with no warning?
4. Destroy, or have no respect for your things?
5. Punch, slap, kick, shove, or bite you?
6. Prevent you from working or attending school?
7. Deny you access to your own money, or money you share as a couple?
8. Force you to have sex against your will?
9. Insult you or call you names?
10. Intimidate, manipulate, or otherwise try to control you or your children?
11. Humiliate you or your kids in front of others?
12. Blame you for his/her temper, stress, drugs, alcohol or other problems?

13. Is he unable or unwilling to get and *keep* a job or
    get training?

*D*omestic violence, whether the abuse is physical, sexual, or emotional, can emotionally scar
you for a long time, and will definitely impact your
children, whether they see you getting abused, or they
are the ones being abused.

If you are in a bad situation, the first goal you should
have is to *leave that situation*! Forget everything else
for right now, and make a safe plan for yourself and
your children.

This plan is one you will make in secret. It will be
your way of having power over the situation. You don't
need permission from your abusive boyfriend, partner,
mother, or father to make this plan. You don't even
necessarily need a dime in your pocket. You just need
good information to make good decisions about what
you will do when you leave.

Do you have friends, family, or other safe people who
can take you and your child in during a time of crisis? If
not, then depending on the severity of the abuse, you
may have to consider going to a safe house or a shelter
the next time he or she becomes violent. Better yet,
don't wait for the next time!

First off, tell someone you trust about the violence.
Develop friendships with neighbors. Ask them to call the
police if they hear suspicious noises coming from your
house, or ask them if they will shelter you for a few
hours or a few nights if you need it. People will surprise
you with kindness if they know you really need help.

Plan your escape, but do it in private. If you are with an abuser, all too often it can become deadly. If a direct confrontation can be avoided, it may save your life, and it will certainly save you some trouble.

Things to Remember

1. Save money, even if you have to hide it, or borrow it.

2. Make sure to take your children, or you may lose them if there is a custody battle.

3. Collect all of your and your children's birth certificates, social security cards, and shot records. Reroute your mail and make an extra set of car keys if you have a car in your name. Hide the keys in an envelope in a P.O. box, or at the home of someone you trust.

4. Learn how to protect yourself, even if you have to learn from a video. Do not fight back unless you feel that your life is in danger.

5. Call 911 during or after an attack. When the police respond, tell them that you want help.

6. Once you are gone, do not call, write, visit, or get in contact with your abuser in any way. It will be a strong temptation, but this is just part of the abuse cycle. Cut them off by using a restraining order if you have to.

For more help with leaving an abusive relationship, read ***Breaking Free from Partner Abuse*** by Mary Marecek (Morning Glory Press).

9

Life Throws
A Curve Ball

My list grew. By the end of one year, "THINGS I WILL DO WITH MY LIFE" had ten things on it. It read:

1. Graduate from college.

2. Get Faith all the lessons she wants: dancing, singing, and gymnastics.

3. Play my trumpet in some shows again.

4. Learn to speak better Spanish.

5. Run my own business (so Faith doesn't have to be in daycare so much).

6. Write a book.

7. Make a cross-country trip to see the places I want to see.

8. Start a savings account.

9. Travel overseas (maybe see Paris?).

10. Live in a house by the beach.

Ten things seemed like a good number to stop with, so I ended my list there. I didn't really think I'd get to do everything on that list, but it was fun to put my dreams down in writing.

Two months after writing down my first dream of going to college, I had applied to several schools, even interviewing at one in Virginia that had housing for single parents. I had my fingers crossed. I knew that it was just a matter of time before I could slip off my waitress apron and slip on a backpack full of college textbooks.

When I got my acceptance letter from college, it was still a shock. It didn't seem real that I was going away to college. I was accepted at the college in Virginia that had eleven apartments on campus specifically for single parents, and a daycare center directly across the driveway from the apartments. My housing and childcare would be included in my tuition program, and financial aid would cover it! I would be able to do work-study for some extra money, and I would be in school full-time.

I proudly told my family, and gladly prepared to leave my boyfriend, who had made sure to tell me how hard it was going to be, and how he "hoped I would make it." He told me to prepare myself to fail, since even people without kids couldn't make it through college sometimes.

I realized I had wasted so much time with this man that I was now chomping at the bit to get going. I only saw potential. My daughter was going to be entering kindergarten at the same time that I would be starting college. We would be living, for the first time, in a place with lots of grass and open fields to play in. I couldn't remember the last time I had been happier.

Unfortunately, just as my life was beginning to change, I got a phone call from a girl named Amber, who told me she was Faith's father's new girlfriend. She called to tell me that Faith's father wanted to be a part of Faith's life, but that he didn't want to call because he knew I'd be angry and upset with him. She told me that they were living together, and that she was wondering if they could take Faith for a visit.

I told her that Faith's father could call me himself, and that I didn't have any idea who she was. I hung up, and a few minutes later he called and said, "What do you want me to do, beg to see my daughter?"

I couldn't believe his nerve! I put Faith in the front room to play, and went out on the porch where I could see her but still talk to him without her listening. I yelled and cussed and screamed at him, and after a while, he just hung up. A little while later he called again, this time with Amber back on the line with him. She told me that she never knew her real father, and that she knew that little girls needed their fathers. She asked again if I would consider letting them come and see Faith.

I told them I would think about it and call them back. As I wrote down their number, I was fuming. Who in the world was this Amber person, and why should I let Faith's father see his daughter after all this time when he couldn't even pick up the phone by himself? He didn't sound apologetic or concerned at all with how she was.

I sat Faith on my lap and asked if she remembered Daddy. She was four and very verbal. She nodded and told me she did. I asked her if she wanted to see him, and she got excited and said, "Oh, yes! I want to see my Daddy!"

So I relented. I called him back and told him that he could come see her. He came by with Amber the next day, and they visited with Faith in my apartment. He acted as if no time had passed, picking Faith up and telling her, "Daddy loves you more than anything!"

Faith was sad when he left. She kept asking for him for days after that visit. Finally, I called him and asked him what he planned to do now. Did he want visitation, and was he planning to start helping me pay for things for Faith? He got upset and told me that he was broke, and didn't have any money to give me, but that he still had the right to see his daughter. I told him that I needed help too, and that he could at least help me with some things for her, like clothes and shoes.

He told me he would do what he could, and then asked me if he could take her to a picnic with some friends. I told him he could, so he came that weekend to pick her up. She was so excited that I began to feel better about letting her go. She wanted to look extra pretty to see her daddy, so I did her hair and let her wear a pretty dress to the picnic.

I spent the day with my boyfriend, and thought to myself that I could get to enjoy having split custody. It gave me some free time without having to burden my parents all the time. By the end of the evening, though, I began to get agitated and hoped that he would bring her back when he said he would.

They arrived on time, but he got out of the car before Faith, and got defensive with me. "Don't go getting all crazy," he said. "She had an accident, but she's fine."

Faith got out of the car with a big sore spot next to her eye. I knelt down beside her and asked her what happened.

"Daddy burned me with his cigarette," she said.

I jumped up and lunged at him. "What?! You burned her with a cigarette!"

"It was an accident!" he yelled at me, getting back in his car.

I knelt beside Faith again. "What happened, Faith? Was it an accident?"

"I met some fun kids and we were running. I ran and ran, and when I ran to Daddy, I ran into his cigarette. But he put water on it and ice on it, and kissed it better, so it only hurts a little, Mommy."

I picked her up and walked inside, leaving him sitting in his car. After a while I watched him drive off. I didn't know what to think when I looked at the burn on Faith's face. My parents had a fit when they saw her, telling me that he wasn't careful enough, and that I was lucky that the cigarette didn't hit her directly in the eye. They also were mad that he was smoking around her, because she got bronchitis very easily.

I found myself defending him to my parents. It was an accident. He didn't mean to burn her. He washed and iced the injury. He was smoking outside with her around, not inside. But still, I felt worried and scared, because now Faith wanted to see him, and I wasn't sure he knew how to take care of an active preschooler.

I did let Faith go with him again after that, although I should have trusted my original instinct. Faith visited his home again and had another accident. This time she was hit in the face with the broken metal rail from a bar stool. The rail hit her over the eye, and ripped the flesh from the middle of her forehead to the bridge of her nose and the top

of her eyelid. She required dozens of stitches to put her
face back together, and was bruised for months after
the incident.

I was horror-struck and blamed myself. I cried for hours
after Faith looked at herself in the mirror and started
screaming, "Monster! I look like an ugly monster!"

The doctors didn't do a very pretty job. They used large
black stitches, not the clear kind they normally use these
days. She looked swollen and was in pain, but the injury
only got worse when she would cry. It took weeks for the
stitches to come out, and years for the scar tissue to turn
from bright pink back to her normal flesh color. Even now,
ten years later, you can see the scars on her face, although,
thankfully, they are not that noticeable.

Her father pretty much disappeared again, although I
heard from him once or twice, at random, over the years. I
was glad for his disappearance this time, and I vowed to
move on with my life, and make my daughter's life better.

The National Center for Injury Prevention and Control reports that more than 900,000 children are
injured each year from abuse or neglect. This number is
only the number of *reported* cases; the actual figures are
much higher. The majority of these children are injured by
a parent or family member. Child neglect accounts for 63
percent of all substantiated cases of child abuse, and is the
most common form of child maltreatment reported to child
protective services.

Neglect is defined as a "type of maltreatment that refers
to the failure to provide needed age-appropriate care." This
includes shelter, food, clothing, education, supervision,
medical care and other basic necessities for development of

physical, intellectual and emotional capacities. Neglect usually has an ongoing pattern of inadequate care.

U.S. Department of Health and Human Services research shows that most parents don't hurt or neglect their children intentionally. Many were themselves abused or neglected.

In addition, very young or inexperienced parents, especially noncustodial parents, may not know how to take care of their babies or what they can reasonably expect from children at different stages of development. Parents who abuse alcohol or other drugs are also more likely to abuse or neglect their children.

I know now I should have insisted that Faith's father spend more time with her in my presence, rather than trusting her safety with him so quickly. I might have realized how unaware he was of safety issues for four-year-olds.

Did You Know . . .

A good way to see hidden danger is to crawl around like a baby?

I wish I had checked out Faith's dad's apartment before I let her go with him. I might have easily spotted dangers that could have caused her injuries.

As strange as it sounds, your home may seem safe, but your baby may be able to find danger that you wouldn't normally see. Crawl around on your hands and knees in your home, and any home where your child is cared for. Get down on the floor and see things from your child's point of view.

Unintentional injuries are the leading cause of death of children 14 years old and under. Injuries at home are the main reason kids under age 3 visit the emergency room. Overall, nearly 70 percent of the children who die from unintentional injuries at home are 4 years old and under.

The most important thing to remember is:

WATCH YOUNG CHILDREN AT ALL TIMES.

Even if your home is child-proofed, it only takes an instant for babies and toddlers to fall, run over to a hot stove, or put the wrong thing in their mouths. No one ever thinks it is going to be their baby that is injured or killed. Know the statistics:

- *130,000 people are treated annually for burns or scalds, and 250 of those die. Two die by being scalded in the bath. (Pediatrics Vol. 116 No. 2)*

- *36,000 children are treated annually for accidental poisoning including weed-killers and insecticides. (Pediatrics Vol. 116 No. 2)*

- *Children drown in puddles and garden pools. A child can drown in only three inches of water.*

- *Thousands of serious accidents to children are caused by makeup and medicines.*

- *Choking causes one in ten deaths in the home.*

If you haven't already done it, get down and crawl around your home. What you find may surprise you!

10

Starting College

I bought an old, ugly car for $500 to drive from Pennsylvania to Virginia where my new school was. My college was small, more like the size of a large high school, but to me it seemed like the biggest place in the world.

My apartment was bigger and nicer than the one I had in Pennsylvania. I felt like I was in a mansion! It had two bedrooms, one and a half bathrooms, a huge eat-in kitchen, and a nice living room. Across the driveway was a football-field-sized lot of land for the kids to play and run in. The school even provided some basic furniture.

The first thing I did when I moved in was put a corkboard up over the desk in the living room and tack my "THINGS I WILL DO WITH MY LIFE" list on it. I had gotten attached to that list. Now, more than ever, I wanted to accomplish the things I had written down.

Faith was excited to have her own room for the first time. I set up her bed and immediately she lay down on it,

trying to get used to the idea that she had her own room.
She went to the small half bathroom and told me that the
little bathroom was hers and the big bathroom was mine. I
told her she still had to use the bathtub, but she said the
sink would be big enough for her to take a bath in. I
laughed with her, and was overjoyed at her excitement.

I took Faith and walked through the apartment building
to meet the other single mothers who lived on campus. I
noticed there were no women there who had more than two
children, and I wondered if that was by accident or if the
college put a cap on the number of children a woman could
bring with her. I didn't remember reading anything about it
in the rules. I imagined it would have been pretty hard to go
to school with three or more children.

Several of the mothers and I formed loose friendships.
We enjoyed each other's company while our kids became
playmates. We all needed help from time to time with
childcare, or stress relief, and talking with others in our
situation helped us keep our sanity.

The most important thing I learned, while being hundreds of miles away from any family or friends, was that
life is much easier if you have a support network. It didn't
take long for all of the single parents there to form a
childcare network. Everyone seemed to help each other out
in some way. Most mothers let each other know when
someone was abusing the system by not giving as much
help as they were requesting.

I learned pretty quickly which parents I wouldn't trust
with my daughter. I sought out positive and loving parents
who, like me, were trying to treat their children like people,
not punching bags. I was shocked at the number of women
who would openly beat their children, and then tell me that

they were hitting the kids because they wanted to make sure their kids "turned out right."

I realized that no one wanted my input on why I thought hitting was wrong, so I learned to keep my mouth shut and steer clear of those parents. I figured they would never link their spankings to their child's continued aggressive and bad behavior. Instead, I sought support from other moms who followed a gentler approach with their children.

Knowing I had some emotional support made it much easier for me to dive into school. I decided I wanted to major in sociology, although I had no real guidance with choosing my major. I chose sociology because I thought I would like to work with people, but I still wasn't sure what career I wanted after college.

I excelled my first year of college, making friends with everyone I could on campus, and soaking up the knowledge I gained from my professors. I got involved in everything I could, and met as many professors and students as possible. I was asked to be Miss SPSS Sweetheart in the Homecoming Court my freshman year, and had fun getting my picture taken in a rhinestone crown and fancy dress.

I loved public speaking, and was overjoyed when I realized I was making almost all As in my classes. I joined the college trivia team, and I got to go to Disney World in Orlando where the competition was being held. My parents came to Virginia and stayed with Faith while I was gone.

It was the first time I got to see what it was like not having a child with me for more than a few hours. I had so much fun! I went to dance clubs and hung out with friends late at night. The funny part was, most of the time I was thinking about Faith and missing her. It was pretty confusing wanting to be part of both those worlds.

Faith was also thriving in our new environment. She had plenty of kids to play with. She and I both loved Miss Lynn, her afternoon daycare teacher, and her new school had a pleasant atmosphere. She also was able to come with me to activities on campus, like basketball games and studying at the library. She adapted to my schedule, and seemed to know when she needed to be quiet or reserved.

Life was not all fun and games, though. It had been a while since I had been in school. I struggled to take good notes and prepare for class. It was hard doing homework late at night after being in school all day and taking care of Faith all evening. I also had to do work study as a require-ment of my financial aid. This meant I had to work on campus, sometimes doing unpleasant things like campus trash cleanup. Life was in constant motion, but the good part was, I didn't have much time to get bored or restless.

At the time, I often wished that I could be a normal college student without the responsibility of a child. Some-times I resented having Faith there with me all the time. My childless friends always had to watch what they said around her, and they never invited me to go out past nine at night. They knew I wouldn't be able to go out to clubs or parties.

I realize now that having Faith with me probably made me a better student. I got enough sleep and stuck to a rigid schedule. After all, my goal was to get a college degree, not go to a college party.

Of course I still noticed guys, especially the older stu-dents. I was lonely, and sometimes I really wanted to date. Between work, classes, homework, and taking care of Faith, however, I didn't have time. I also got a bad reaction from a few guys who chatted it up with me, *until* I mentioned I lived in single-parent housing.

This reaction from guys bothered me at first, until I realized that I was proud of myself for being a college student and a single mom. I wasn't going to let anyone or anything make me feel bad about it.

I was learning and doing new things in a way that was nothing like high school. I felt busy, and sometimes overwhelmed, but it was a different kind of overwhelmed than I had experienced before. It was an "I'll do something with my life if I can just hang on" kind of overwhelmed.

My money was tight because I could only work part-time, but since my housing and daycare were covered by my tuition, it was manageable. Some of the girls got food stamps and welfare, and they would help me out with food if they saw that things were getting really tight for me.

I could have qualified for food stamps also, but I was now worried about Social Services providing my daughter's father with our information. I went to the office with one of the other mothers to see if I could get some help. They told me that, because I wasn't getting child support, they would need to find Faith's dad and make him pay.

I decided that I did not want the hassle of that. I knew that Faith's dad would not be happy to have to pay me child support after all these years, especially if I was getting it so I could better my life. I didn't want him trying to get back in contact with me and Faith and adding anything negative to our lives. The thought frightened me so badly that I didn't go back to the welfare office after that. Instead, I got WIC, and stocked up on eggs, peanut butter, cereal, and milk, and made these things the staples of our diet.

I let him off the hook from being responsible, and Faith and I suffered because of it. It was a foolish move on my part, one that I now regret.

Is College for You?

*I*s college for you? Having a minimum-wage job
  can be great for after-school or as part-time work
or starting in the job market.

But is serving up fries or cleaning offices what you
would choose to do eight hours a day for the next 30 or 40
years? Probably not. Unless you get more than a high-
school education, though, it will be difficult for you to get
more than a minimum-wage job.

In this century, employers say, education beyond high
school and the skills learned there are essential. Since this
is when you'll be entering the job market, that's you and
your job skills they're talking about. A four-year college is
not the only choice for education. On-the-job training,
apprenticeships, community college, or vocational schools
can give you the education you need to make a better wage.

Getting ready for a college education requires a lot of
time, effort, and careful planning. But college also provides
information and skills that you will use for the rest of your
life to help you succeed in whatever you do. Staying in
school and going to college will help you:

1. Get a better job. More and more jobs require education beyond high school. With a college education,
   you'll have more jobs from which to choose.

2. Earn more money. A person who goes to college
   usually earns more than a person who doesn't. On
   average, over a lifetime, someone who spends two
   years in college earns $250,000 more than someone
   who doesn't. That's right — a quarter of a million
   dollars more over a lifetime.

3. *Get a good start in life. College also trains you to organize and express your thoughts clearly, make informed decisions, and use technology — all useful skills on and off the job and for life.*

Many teenagers do not go to college because they don't enjoy high school. What they don't realize is that college is very different from high school. College professors don't give detention or monitor students like a high school teacher. They allow you to be responsible for your success or failure.

College also allows you to choose the types of classes you want to take. You choose your career (major), and after taking some basic education courses, about the only classes you take are the ones you need to develop the skills required for the job, and ultimately, the life you want for yourself.

Even if you never thought about going to college before, you may find you need it to reach your goals. Look into it with an open mind. College can be a good way to change your life.

Did You Know . . .

No matter what your goal, college may help?

If you're thinking college is not for you, perhaps because you think you won't like it, please reconsider. Remember that the average annual salary for a person who has earned a two-year Associate's degree is $33,400 as compared to $26,200 for a high school graduate, according to the U.S. Department of Commerce. Average annual salary for someone with a four-year Bachelor's degree is $42,200.

Community colleges are low cost, and are a good starting point for many single parents. Many community colleges will even allow a student to enroll before the age of 18, if they have a GED (General Education Development certificate). Sometimes, even minors without a GED or diploma can secure a special admission to a community college. You can find out if you qualify by discussing your circumstances with an admissions counselor. For instance, you might work on your GED or high school diploma at the same time as taking college courses.

You may find it advantageous to attend a community college first whether or not you plan to graduate from a four-year university. Is a community college located near you? If you don't think you can get to a university right now, learn about the opportunities at your local community college.

On p. 154 in the Appendix, you will find ten examples of some of the possible jobs for which you could qualify by earning a two-year AA (Associate of Arts) degree from a community college. There are hundreds of others.

You can also receive short-term training from most community colleges. A tremendous number of these certificate programs are offered at various institutions. If you know you want a better or a different job than the one you have now and/or are qualified for, contact the Career Development Center at your community college. You'll find training there as good as or better than that offered at private training facilities, and classes at the community college will almost always be a great deal less expensive.

Go to <www.lamabooks.com> for resource information. This site offers a directory for California which lists the state's 108 community colleges and the 254 programs available in 13 different vocational areas throughout the state of California. You may be able to find a similar directory available for your state.

However, if you need money to cover housing, there is usually no housing on a community college campus, so financial aid may not cover that expense even if you are in school full-time. By getting your GED or diploma first, or by transferring from a community college, you can go to a four-year college where you may find on-campus housing and daycare.

See the Appendix, pages 159-164, for a description of some of the colleges in various parts of the United States that have single parent housing programs.

The admissions process to a four-year school is tougher, but you may get enough financial aid to cover housing, food, tuition and childcare. Financial aid makes it easier for your *job* to be a college student. Your aid is your "income," which allows you to work fewer hours to cover your expenses.

If you can do without a car while you are in school, you may even be able to live solely off your financial aid, if you budget your money carefully. Having no car will cut out big expenses, like car insurance, gas, and maintenance.

The U.S. Department of Education provides more than $40 billion in aid for college students each year. Being from a low- or middle-income family should never keep anyone from going to college. Every year, more than half of all students in college receive some type of financial aid.

Students with children are considered independent in college, so you'll be able to get federal grants and loans on your own. Be sure to fill out the FAFSA (Free Application for Federal Student Aid) at the same time you're filling out college applications.

You can find the FAFSA form at any high school or college guidance office, at your local library, or on the internet at <www.fafsa.ed.gov> You'll need your tax return and social security number.

After you've been accepted by your college, write out your expected expenses for daycare, food, housing, books, tuition, and school supplies. Go visit the college's financial aid office. They can help you get the amount you need to pay for tuition and expenses while you are in school.

For the most up-to-date information about federal

financial aid, contact the U.S. Department of Education at: 1-8OO-USA-LEARN, or 1-8OO-4FED-AID.

Don't go to school without a plan! This would waste your time and money. Research what you want to major in and stick to it. Then see if anyone is offering grants (free money) to students with your major and/or to women or single parent students.

Use the Internet! Look online for grants and services. Women's organizations are also a valuable resource for female students.

11

Traveling the World As a Single Parent

*B*y the start of the second semester, I could barely remember my old life. I found my niche in school, and had figured out how to balance parenting with school and work. I also began trying to knock things off my "THINGS I WILL DO WITH MY LIFE" list.

I brought my old high school trumpet with me to college. I dusted it off, and started playing in the jazz and pep bands. I was very fond of the music professor. He was patient and motivating. He made me *feel* the music I played, and my proficiency improved greatly under his watch. He made me find the gentle, subtle tones in my instrument, and I felt wonderful when I played, even if the neighbors in my building didn't. The professor let Faith sit in on practices, and she was allowed to ride with me on the bus when we played for games and competitions. Playing with the school band knocked number 3 off my goal list: *Play my trumpet in some shows again.*

I also took a Spanish class, although it was a little too basic to fulfill number 4: *Learn to speak better Spanish.* My parents both speak Spanish, so it was embarrassing that even my "Spanglish" was bad. I really wanted to get better, but my college Spanish class wasn't going to accomplish that. I was mentioning my frustration over my Spanish skills to a friend when one of my classmates popped his head in on our conversation. "You should do a study-abroad," he said. "They have short programs for the summer. Maybe your parents could watch your daughter so you could go for a semester or a year program."

Study-abroad had never entered my mind before. I didn't even know what it was. I knew that I didn't want to leave my daughter, not even for one semester, so I kept the thought in the back of my mind for several months.

The thought only resurfaced after I had an incredibly vivid dream one night.

I was with Faith walking down a cobblestone road. I waved to a woman and spoke to her in Spanish. She spoke back to me and I understood her, then I turned and used a key to go inside a hacienda style house. Our things were inside, so it was obviously our house. I gathered some mail and opened two large balcony doors that opened to a courtyard. Faith started pulling clothes from a line in the courtyard and turned around to smile at me.

Then I woke up.

The dream lingered because it was so vivid. I could remember the smells, the temperature, and the person I spoke to. I remembered the fabric of the curtains, and the layout of the house. That dream in itself would have probably passed and been forgotten, if it weren't for what happened next.

Someone knocked on my door.

When I opened it, I was surprised to see the classmate who had discussed studying abroad with me months earlier. He had never been to my apartment before, although it was a small campus and I was easy enough to find.

When I asked him why he was visiting, he said, "I brought you some study abroad pamphlets. I requested some for myself months ago for France, but these came in the mail today. They're for Spain, so I thought you might like them."

Wow!

That's the thought that went through my mind.

Wow!

I could have just been reading into things, or I could have been getting a message from above, but from that moment on I felt I was meant to go to Spain.

I was sitting on the couch across from the corkboard that held my list, staring at the pamphlets in my hand when I absentmindedly thought to myself, "I could knock number 4 and number 9 off my list if I go to Spain!"

I went across the hall to talk to my friend Robin. I told her about my dream, and about my friend bringing me the pamphlets.

She said, "Sounds like God is talking, if you feel like listening."

I thought about that for a while, and then ran into another single mother on campus. This mother's goal was to be a singer. She was the mother of two boys, yet still went to competitions all over the United States to perform. She was trying to live her dream of becoming a professional singer, and I wanted to know what she thought.

She surprised me by saying, "You're crazy if you go to

Europe and take Faith with you, and you're crazy if you go
and leave her with your parents. I would never do that to
my kids."

I had my doubts, and knew it was scary to leave the
country, but I really felt that it was the right thing for me to
do. My family was divided on the issue as well. My sister
told me to go and she would take my daughter, but I knew I
could never go away that long without my child. My father
was also worried, but my mother told me that I had only
one life to live, and she was proud of me for living it.

Sometimes it just takes one person to give you the right
bit of encouragement (or discouragement) that makes the
difference between forgetting your dream or feeling confident enough to live out that dream. Without my mother's
words, I might have decided against going to Europe. But
that didn't happen. After researching, calling, planning, and
working extra jobs to earn the money I needed, I decided to
enroll at the University of Granada in Spain. I was going
to be the first person from my college to study abroad
with a child.

Six months later I arrived in London for a short visit
before heading to my host-home in Granada, Spain.
The airport was a madhouse! There were huge lines and
bustling people everywhere. I held onto Faith's hand tightly
as we tried to figure out how to get to our hotel. I stepped
outside and commented to a woman standing near the exit,
"Is this always so crazy?"

She shook her head and said in a strong English accent,
"'Fraid not. Everybody just wants to get a look at Princess
Diana's funeral."

That's how I found out that, as I was packing for my first

trip to England, the rest of the world was listening to news about the death of Princess Diana in France.

As I found my shuttle to the airport and loaded my bags, I listened as travelers from around the world came through Heathrow airport to pay tribute to the Princess. Driving by Buckingham Palace, the shuttle driver apologized for the delay, saying that thousands of people were clogging the streets to leave flowers at the Abbey for her funeral. I took advantage of the standstill traffic and got out of the shuttle to take a quick look around.

The rest of my visit consisted of the neighborhood where my hotel was. I watched the news in a restaurant where I had dinner with Faith, and then my jetlagged body fell asleep before dark. Faith woke me up in the middle of the night, scared because she didn't know where she was. So I sang her favorite song to her, and she fell back asleep until morning.

We had limited time before we had to meet our group at the airport the next day. I felt nervous, because I knew that none of the other college students would have kids. As I walked over and met the group, I immediately noticed them. They all looked like typical, well-to-do, American college students. They looked right through me, thinking that I was just a mom traveling with her kid, not a college student going to the University with them.

I sat down, and Faith immediately started talking to one of the female students sitting next to us. "Hi, we're going to Granada. We're in college there."

The girl looked at me, and said, "You're American?"

I nodded, "Yeah, I'm doing a study abroad for a semester. I'm only staying with a host family for two weeks, until I can find an apartment there. This is my daughter, Faith."

Several other people joined in the conversation, commenting on "how brave" I was and "how cute" Faith was. Someone asked me what "nationality" I was, so I said "American," not realizing right away that he was wondering because, being biracial Black and Puerto-Rican, I have a "different" kind of look to me.

I felt a little like a sideshow event, even though Faith loved the attention. After the conversation died down, I moved over to another area. I scanned the group. I wondered if I was trying to cross too many barriers, being basically poor, being a single parent, and being nonwhite. I definitely noticed that there was no one there with a child, of course, but there were three African American girls, two Hispanic girls, and one Hispanic guy. They seemed to be mingling with the group okay, so I stopped for a minute, composed myself, and thought positive thoughts as I boarded the plane.

I had no doubts and no problems making friends with the other students after I got to Spain. The town was beautiful . . . the people were beautiful . . . and I stood around for most of the first week with my mouth open.

I wanted to see castles, and castles I saw. Castles and cathedrals are what Spain is all about. Before I even started classes, I visited museums and plazas. I saw Gypsies and flamenco dancers in the park. I got used to cobblestone sidewalks and the loud "vroom" of the scooters that people rode through the narrow streets.

There were dozens of shops lining the streets of each neighborhood. Apparently no one shopped in large quantities at a supermarket. Instead, they shopped each day, buying their food fresh from each of the small shops that sold fruit, meat, or breads separately.

That became my life too. After two weeks with a host family, I found an apartment. My apartment, whether it was a subconscious choice or a fateful coincidence, looked remarkably like the one I had dreamed about months earlier.

Faith began first grade at the local *colegio*. She couldn't speak a word of Spanish at first, and my Spanish was terrible, but we somehow got her enrolled, and figured out her daily schedule of class in the morning, then home for siesta, then class again in the evening.

It rained every day in Spain. It never lasted long, though. Just enough to wet the ground, and then the clouds moved on. I enjoyed the rain, and got used to bringing an umbrella everywhere I went. I got close to a few friends. Amanda and Diara were two of the African American girls I saw at the airport, and Gaby was Panamanian, but lived in California and went to the University of California, San Diego. We bonded, and spent most days together for at least some point in time.

Gaby helped me with baby-sitting, and in return I helped her out with a few bucks from time to time. I also had my own apartment, so people came to visit or stay the night when they were annoyed with their host families.

I dated while I lived in Spain, as well. Jouness was Moroccan and lived in Europe for athletic competitions in which he participated. He lived with a friend named Abdel, a small wiry athlete who would have philosophical and intellectual conversations with me about the world for hours. Perhaps if Abdel's brain were inserted in Jouness' body, the relationship would have lasted longer.

My priority, however, was school. I loved taking my classes completely in Spanish. I had my dictionary open a lot at first, but later I understood my professors well, and began to actively participate in class.

Jouness spoke no English, so dating him helped me improve my Spanish, since it was the only language in which we could communicate. Faith had far exceeded my language skills after only three months. I had labeled everything in the house with a Spanish name tag, so if she wanted something, she had to ask for it in Spanish.

My money stretched surprisingly far. Financial aid paid for tuition, books, and educational trips. I had also worked like crazy the summer before my trip to raise as much money as I could. I worked in a water-testing lab, cleaning test tubes. I painted apartments, baby-sat, and waited tables part-time.

I read that I could find a nice apartment in Spain for about 300 American dollars per month, so I budgeted for housing, food, travel, and incidentals, and left for Spain with about $3,800 in the bank. That was more money than I had ever seen at that time, but I knew I had to be careful with it.

Life in Spain was simple and no frills. We washed our clothes in our tiny bathtub. We heated water on our stove with small butane tanks that I was terrified to use at first, for fear of blowing up the building. Laundromats were virtually impossible to find, and if you did, they were expensive. There was no air conditioning or heaters in my building, only a small space heater that warmed one room at a time.

Most locals did not use the one commercialized grocery store in town. Only people with money, or tourists used it.

However, there I could find some items that I was used to, like fresh milk. I rarely went there for anything else because of the expense. Their meat section included rows of dead rabbits hanging by their ears on the wall, and Faith was traumatized by it. She would walk around the meat section with her eyes closed so she wouldn't have to see the dead bunnies.

Thanksgiving rolled around and, of course, it is not celebrated in Spain. I was disappointed that there was no turkey, mashed potatoes, or pumpkin pie. Instead, Faith and I, with a group of other Americans from school, went to a restaurant and ate a meal that couldn't compare to the huge feast I was used to my mother making. I got a little homesick then, and couldn't wait to go back and visit my parents over Christmas.

After a couple of months in Spain, I decided that one semester wasn't long enough. During my visit to the United States for Christmas, I made plans to try to stretch my dollars and make them last for the year. My apartment cost less than I anticipated, at around 200 American dollars per month, and I really felt I wanted to travel a bit more around Europe, so I decided to stay for another semester.

When I returned to Granada after Christmas, I became an expert bargain traveler. I saw much of Spain. Madrid was like the New York City of Spain. Sevilla was quaint and beautiful. Marbella sat on the Mediterranean Sea. I saw dozens of other towns, cities, and ruins, all with Faith by my side.

In my travels, I rented a car and drove to Gibraltar, which is located at the southern tip of Spain, yet owned by the United Kingdom. It was very strange driving into a "little Britain," and hearing people speak English after so many months of hearing only Spanish. Gibraltar is one place that I would recommend to anyone to see. The rock of Gibraltar cannot be described with words. You have to see it to grasp how beautiful it is.

In March, during a short break at my college in Granada, I went to Paris. I felt completely overwhelmed by not being able to understand any French. I didn't even know how to say bathroom! I realized that I didn't prepare myself for that visit at all. Therefore it was not fun, only uncomfortable and a little scary.

I vowed to myself that I would return again one day, after having prepared myself with some basic language skills. Faith got homesick while there, so I asked the airline if I could fly standby for a reasonable price to the United States. I left from Paris to visit my family. That was the visit where I saw Jane in the parking lot of the bank.

During my visit, I drove to Virginia to get some things from my apartment there. It was then that the housing office dropped a bombshell on me: I had lost my housing and daycare on campus for the following year, because of my decision to stay in Spain another semester.

I was devastated. I didn't know how I could afford housing and daycare and still go to school full-time. I went back to Granada, requested my grades from the previous semester, and packed up my apartment. I went back to the United States to figure out what I was going to do about college.

Luckily Faith was in school during the day, so I was okay without daycare, but someone had moved into my apartment at school. They had been told to move in with all of my things still in the apartment. As I went to get my belongings, I was furious that some of my items had been used and broken. I was so upset!

I had to make a new plan for myself. I was going to be a junior in college, and I wanted to graduate on time! Even though I was angry about how my housing had been handled, I decided quickly to make arrangements to go to another college so I wouldn't miss a semester.

The school in Virginia let me enroll in classes that March, even though the semester was nearly half over. One of the single parents at the school let me stay with her temporarily, to finish the semester before I left.

Devastated as I was about my living arrangement, I didn't regret my decision to go to Europe. I had lived out two of my dreams. I could speak enough Spanish to hold conversations, and I was proud of myself for that. I had visited London and Paris, and studied in Spain.

I dated and made friends with people from dozens of other countries and cultures. Along the way, I gave people a new image of what it meant to be a single mom. I wasn't sitting at home complaining about money or the things I couldn't do. I was planning my future just like they were, and I had a happy, well-adjusted daughter.

When a single parent travels with a child, the first concern is keeping both parent and child safe. In many countries, a woman traveling alone with a child feels out of place and may appear an easy target for thieves.

Being confident and knowing a few key things about how not to "look like a tourist" can make the difference in how your travel experience goes. If you are fumbling with a map, looking confused, and reading a language dictionary, you may as well put a sign on you that says, "Rob me, my travelers checks are in my fanny pack."

The benefits of traveling far outweigh the risks. Women

traveling with their children can have closer relationships with them. You learn about yourself and what kind of person your child is. Besides, you can be the only single mother on your block who knows how much forty American dollars is in Irish pounds, how to take the Eurail train from France to Germany, and how to order tapas in Madrid without sounding like an uncultured American.

Traveling gives you a new appreciation for life by showing you that you are just one tiny piece of a world that is full of thousands of different cultures and life-styles. It can give you a whole new perspective on your life, and on what things are truly important.

Educate yourself! Learn the local customs and how to dress, and do not wear expensive jewelry or keep your camera strapped around your neck. Be sure your children know the name of your hotel or have the hotel name taped to them. Read about the bus or subway schedules in advance, and study your maps of the area. Involve your child and make a game of it!

You may not be interested in going to Europe, but you probably have another dream just as big. I was surprised when my friends and family told me they thought my idea to study abroad was a bad one. I thought they would be thrilled at my desire to go to Spain. Unfortunately, many people won't understand or support a dream you have for yourself if it is hard for them to see themselves doing it.

If you want to do something outside the norm, be sure to research it, and make sure it is realistic for you to accomplish with your child by your side. You obviously don't want to put yourself or your child in a dangerous situation.

Whatever your goal or your dream . . . plan . . . plan . . . and plan some more. *Then go do it.*

Did You Know . . .

There are study abroad options specifically for people with children?

I know that many young moms would find the idea of traveling alone to a foreign country with their children to be more of a nightmare than a dream. But, for those parents wanting to learn a new language while experiencing life overseas, there are now more options.

Some programs have recognized the need for accommodations for parents in their foreign language study-abroad schools. It's a real option for single parents who want the experience of going to another country and learning valuable language skills. Some programs you pay for yourself; others (if used for college credit) can be paid for with financial aid. The following three websites can provide you with detailed information on a variety of programs: <www.languagesabroad.com> <www.adventuresabroad.com> <www.singleparenttravel.net>

Providing your children with the opportunity to see other countries and cultures can be an invaluable gift. However, when planning your trip, remember *they are still going to behave like children.* Be sure to do research to learn if the destination is family friendly.

Once you've decided on a destination, get a globe and show your child where he or she is going. Explain that people use a different language, and that things will look different. Practice some words in the country's language.

Mentally prepare yourself and your children for the change, and get your passports early!

12

Setbacks Happen

I made the decision to leave Virginia and move in with my parents while I enrolled in a State University in Pennsylvania. I stayed with my parents long enough to get a job and find a new place to live. They didn't charge me for rent or food. By letting me save all of my money for a new apartment, they made my transition much easier. I knew they were proud of me for enrolling right back in school and not letting the problem at my other college stop me from missing a semester.

My new college was huge in comparison to my first one, but after living in Europe, I was ready for that transition. I felt confident and prepared from my experiences, even though my classes were tougher, and I had to work a forty-hour week to make ends meet.

I got a job at the YWCA, and worked around my college schedule. Through the YWCA, I got free childcare and summer camp for Faith. I also got a part-time job working at a group home for pregnant and parenting teens.

My work at the group home was probably tougher than any job I've ever held — but not because of my job duties. It was hard emotionally, seeing these girls who reminded me of the old me, from a time before I started believing that I could do and be a little bit more.

The hardest part was hearing girl after girl tell me about her experience of being abused, physically, emotionally, and sexually, either at home, or by a boyfriend. There were girls as young as thirteen who had gotten pregnant, usually by men much older than they were. Many of the girls did poorly in school, and didn't know how to read very well. Often they didn't have a parent who read to them or helped them in school when they were younger. As a result, most of the girls didn't seem to have hope for their future.

I hid the fact that I went to Europe and was in college from these girls at first. It was such a strange reaction from me, but I felt bad flaunting my good experiences in front of them, when most of them believed they had little to look forward to. I didn't want to make them feel worse about their situation. I was warned by the counselors not to discuss my personal life with the girls, and I heeded their advice.

There was one young girl in the program, Becky, who had tried to commit suicide the week before I arrived. She was sixteen, and her son was only a couple of weeks old when she began having some episodes of psychosis. I didn't really understand what was wrong with her, and had just recently begun learning about mood disorders in college and at work. She seemed crazy at times, and was taking medication for help.

I never realized how lucky Faith and I were to have gone through my pregnancy hormonal problems almost un-scathed. I was fatigued, distant, and had my confused moments, but didn't realize that pregnancy can cause some dangerous hormonal mood disorders. I also didn't know that hormonal problems can be especially difficult in pregnant teenagers.

Becky was a late bloomer. She got her period at fifteen, and shortly afterward she got pregnant. The head counselor at the group home told me that might have been a key reason for her onset of postpartum psychosis. After a couple of months, Becky seemed fine, and her symptoms lessened. She continued counseling and medication throughout my time there.

As my relationships with the girls continued, I felt more compelled to discuss my experiences as a teen mother. I could not understand why it was so frowned upon to dis-cuss my personal situation with the girls, especially since I was the only counselor working at the home that had experienced teen parenthood. I felt I had some relevant advice to give. Many of these girls were wards of the state and would be sent out on their own at eighteen years of age, with no idea of what they would do.

I began talking to some of the older girls about their options for work, daycare and college, and told them I was a single mother in college. I told all of them that I would be glad to help anyone with filling out paperwork for college and applying for financial aid.

One girl, Olive, was getting ready to graduate and leave the group home, and wasn't sure what to do with her life. I told her to get everything together and I would help her try

to apply to college as quickly as possible. She was bright
and made good grades, but she was told that her son would
be put in foster care when she left the home if she couldn't
prove she could care for him on her own.

This was the story for many of the girls. The counselors
in the program had the power to report to the state if they
felt a girl could not get a job, an apartment, and adequate
childcare for her child. The girl would have to leave the
home after high-school without her child, and the state
would put her child in foster care until she proved she was
able to provide for the child.

Olive showed a special interest in college, but was afraid
of losing her son if she decided to go. She told me that no
one had ever given her enough information for her to
realize she might be able to go to college. She said she
really wanted to be a lawyer, and help young girls like her
to have more rights. She told me how she had been
bounced from foster home to foster home after her mother's
death, and how her father never tried to get her when she
was placed in a home.

She said that she ended up in the group home after
becoming pregnant at 14 and fighting off a foster father that
was molesting her. She said no one believed her because
she didn't say anything until after she was arrested for
hitting him with a telephone. She said that she couldn't
wait to get out on her own and do something with her life.
I gave Olive my phone number, and told her that I would
help her get her college applications together in my
free time.

The next day when I went to work, I was called into the
office. The head counselor there handed me the piece of

paper that I had given Olive the day before, and repri-
manded me for getting personally involved with the girls.

I tried to explain that I was simply going to help her get
her paperwork in before college deadlines, so she could
make a better life for her and her son, but the counselor
wouldn't let me finish.

"What Olive needs to keep her son is a good job and a
decent apartment, not college."

I told her that I was in college, and that student loans
paid for part of my living expenses, and that I was a single
mother. I tried to explain that Olive was looking for schools
that had apartment housing and childcare onsite. I told her
that Olive would always be struggling if she just got a job
and an apartment and didn't gain some more skills. I argued
that she was different, more driven, and brighter in school
than many of the other girls.

The head counselor told me that I could not relate my
college success to what Olive was capable of. She told me
that the only reason I was successful was because I had my
parents. She told me that I was going to be the one held
responsible when Olive spent her time looking for a college
rather than an apartment and job, and therefore would not
get custody of her son. She told me that I was the type of
person that made it necessary to have the rule against
discussing our personal lives with the girls.

I was shocked. I didn't feel that discussing options and
giving encouragement to the girls was detrimental. I
worked my shift, said goodbye to the girls, and resigned
later that week. Several months later I ran into someone
from work who told me Olive moved into a halfway house,
and then got a job, an apartment, and custody of her son.

Not long after finding out that news, I began to get strange hang-up phone calls in the middle of the night. Finally, after a few such calls, I heard Olive's voice at the end of the line. She sounded flat and depressed. Her voice sounded so hopeless and worn-out that it scared me.

"I moved in with this guy I met, so I could have an apartment to keep my son. But he raped me and I had to go to a shelter. I was scared they were going to take my baby away, so I moved to New York. I tried to find my dad, but his new wife told me I can't stay with them."

I asked Olive where she was now, and how I could help her, but she hung up. I called the operator and asked them if they could trace the call, and they directed me to the police department. The police told me they couldn't trace it for me under the circumstances, and I was left frustrated and unable to find out where the call came from.

I never heard from Olive again, but I have wondered about her for a long time. That strange phone call has haunted me to this day. Olive's voice had an unemotional and detached "I've lost all hope" tone.

I hope Olive didn't do anything drastic that night. Unfortunately, I know her scars are long and deep. I pray she escaped the cycle. I hope to this day that she and her child are all right.

Special Challenges
of Having a Baby Before Age 18

If you're 17 or younger, you probably already know that you can't apply for TANF (Temporary Aid for Needy Families) by yourself, and that there are strict rules about how you receive any of those funds, who you live with, requirements concerning going to school or being enrolled in job training, etc.

If you're under 16, you can't drive your baby to the doctor — even if you have a car.

You probably can't rent an apartment by yourself because in many states a minor cannot sign a rental contract.

Laws vary from state to state. Learn your state's laws for filing for paternity, applying for aid, and other benefits. Find out what you can do while you're under 18, and what the law in your state says you can't.

Parents and extended family can be a big help. The girls in the home where I worked had no family willing to support them. Sadly, in this particular home, residents received no support for furthering their education and increasing their job skills.

If this is your situation, you probably feel like you're between a rock and a hard place. No matter how adorable your baby is, you may be having a tough time even thinking about your dreams, let alone following them.

*Probably the best thing you can do is stay in school. If your school has no special program, and you have no one to take care of your baby, home teaching or independent study might work for you. Whatever you do, figure out a way to continue your education, improve your reading skills, and **PLAN what you will do when you turn 18.***

Did You Know . . .

That everyone feels overwhelmed at some point?

Everyone has had a time in their life when they feel overwhelmed. If you begin to feel upset to the point that you are feeling desperate, call someone and talk to them. The following are numbers you can call to talk to someone who can help in almost any crisis. You can make these calls anonymously if you choose.

The National Suicide Hotline
1-800-784-2433

If you ever feel so hopeless that you are considering committing suicide . . . call them. Death is permanent, final, and irreversible. Your current situation, no matter how bad, is only temporary!

RAINN (Rape Abuse and Incest National Network)
National Rape Crisis Hotline
1-800-656-4673

If you are the victim of a rape, or know someone who needs help, call the rape hotline to find a safe person to talk to.

National Child Safety Council Childwatch Hotline
1-800-222-1464

Answers questions and distributes literature on safety, including drug abuse, household dangers, and electricity.

National Domestic Violence/
Child Abuse/ Sexual Abuse Hotline
1-800-799-SAFE

This is a great resource for anyone — man, woman or child — who is experiencing or has experienced domestic violence or abuse, or who suspects that someone they know is being abused.

National Youth Crisis Hotline
1-800-442-HOPE

Provides counseling and referrals to local drug treatment centers, shelters, and counseling services. Responds to youth dealing with pregnancy, molestation, suicide, and child abuse. Operates 24 hours, seven days a week.

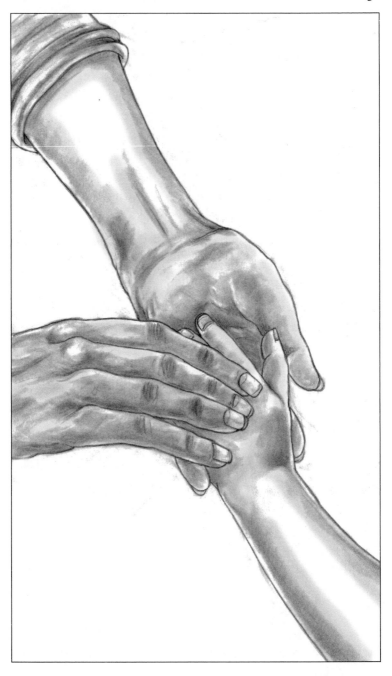

13

Life
After College

After leaving work at the group home, I went back to work at one of the restaurants where I waited tables before I started college. I began going to college year-round so I could get out more quickly. I started the summer after I returned from Spain and went to school straight through, fall, winter, spring, summer, and fall again.

Finally, in December, I graduated with a B.A. in sociology with over a 3.0 grade point average. It took exactly three years and three months to knock the Number One thing off my "THINGS I WILL DO WITH MY LIFE" list.

I graduated from college, traveled and studied in three countries, and made good grades, all while working and taking care of my child. I was no longer sitting on my front stoop waiting to see if any neighborhood gossip would be the highlight of my day. I was proud of myself and was excited to see what life had in store for me after college.

However, even though life was better, as Faith got older,

she was still struggling with questions about her father. As hard as I worked to give her everything I could, she still needed to know, and nothing I did could change that. I had no idea where he was, but I did know where his family lived. I told Faith that if she wanted to meet her father's family, I would take her to meet them.

Faith wasn't too sure how she felt about meeting her father's family, but I assured her that they would love to see her, and that they had always tried to keep in touch. She knew that cards and presents would come from them in the mail from time to time, but she didn't feel a bond with them. I felt that it was time for her to try to establish a relationship with them. I realized that this was important to her. She needed to know who "the other half" of her was.

I called her great-grandmother one evening, and was surprised to hear how strong she sounded in her 90s. Sharp as a tack, she knew me right away, and told me that she wanted to see Faith. She said she would get the family together at her house for a party. I decided to drive the 12-hour trip.

I borrowed a video camera so Faith could capture her adventure on tape. We left at 4:30 a.m. in my faithful Volkswagen. It was dark, but we were wide-awake, ready to see the sights on our long trip.

We arrived late that evening at Faith's great-grandmother's house, exhausted after driving through three states and getting in one minor car accident. The family was all there with balloons and presents, so happy to see Faith. They told me how much they appreciated me bringing Faith to see them, and let me know that they wanted a real relationship with her. Faith was overwhelmed by all of this, and was gripping my side out of shyness and fear as everyone introduced themselves.

Shockingly, one of the people who introduced themselves was her father. I didn't recognize him because he was bald and had put weight on his previously skinny frame. Faith was a little in shock and whispered, "You said he had long hair!"

The more relaxed I was, the easier it was for Faith to get to know the people with whom she shared a bloodline. Slowly, as time passed, Faith loosened her grip on my leg and warmed up to everyone.

Eventually she sat down beside her father. He was shocked at how tall she was. He kept staring as though he couldn't figure out how the tiny baby we had together had turned into this beautiful preteen girl. Faith told him he was "nice," and then told him about her school and her friends.

I wasn't sure how I'd feel to see him, but I realized I wasn't angry with him anymore. I realized that my life was good, and that it was he who had missed out on all those years with Faith.

Unfortunately, after that day, Faith never got to see her father again. He called and wrote, and sent money for a few months, but she never saw him face to face. Then, without warning, he slipped back out of her life with no word as to why.

Faith was more devastated by this second disappearing act than she was by all the other years that she didn't see him. I tried to explain it the best way I knew, but I didn't understand it myself.

But other family members, like Faith's grandmother and her husband, have stayed in contact since our meeting. Faith's uncle, wife, and their kids visit, send letters, and make sure Faith knows she is family. Her aunt and her children also became familiar faces during our visits as well. I was determined to let Faith have the other side of her family, with or without her father's involvement. He might not be there for her, but I was not going to take away her whole family.

I realized how important it was to let my daughter have a complete history, and how significant bloodlines are to people. I am glad we made that trip, and that we continue to visit, and get visits, from her extended family. I am glad that even though Faith didn't have a father most of her life, she still gets to have his family.

Your child will have questions about his/her father whether s/he has visitation or a relationship with him or not. Children want and need to know who their biological parents are, and they do better socially and academically when they have a positive relationship with both parents.

If the father voluntarily signs a "Declaration of Paternity" form, his fatherhood is automatically assumed. This will allow you to collect child support without going to court. If you are awarded child support, the father will probably have a right to visit the child as well. In fact, he probably has that right even if he doesn't provide for his child's financial support.

Did You Know . . .

Paternal grandparents have rights?

Even if your child doesn't know, visit, or have a relationship with his or her father, it doesn't mean that the grandparents, aunts, uncles, and cousins don't want a relationship. Often these family members are victims of the choices that the parent makes.

Your child's father's family could offer a link to heritage, ancestors, and physical makeup. They can offer your child a feeling of wholeness, and extend your support base as you raise your child alone. I suggest trying to mend fences with your child's other family, and keeping a relationship with them as s/he grows.

Always be concerned that animosity between you and your child's grandparents, which is openly displayed in the presence of the child, is harmful. A visiting grandparent might express negative thoughts toward you, in regard to your parenting and/or lifestyle. It's up to you to keep your cool and let the grandparent know that you are learning and studying as much as you can about parenting, because you want to be the best parent you can be. Don't let them ruffle your feathers!

Letting grandparents know how important it is that you have a good relationship with them for the sake of your child can go a long way. Having your child know how much you like and respect her grandparents can help her grow to feel good about herself and secure in her family.

Above all else, don't blame the entire family for the father's mistakes, or vice versa.

14

Epilogue

It's not the list, it's what you accomplish from the list.

A couple of years after I graduated, my "THINGS I WILL DO WITH MY LIFE" list was looking worn and tattered. Its new home was with me in San Diego, California. I relocated there after visiting Gaby, who I met in Spain. She graduated from college and invited me to see her in Southern California, where she was working on a Master's degree. I fell in love with San Diego, and began making plans to move there.

The beat up piece of yellow legal paper on which I had written my goals had seen better days, but I could not bring myself to rewrite the list on a new piece of paper. The ten-item list still read:

1. Graduate from college.

2. Get Faith all the lessons she wants: dancing, singing, and gymnastics.

3. Play my trumpet in some shows again.

4. Learn to speak better Spanish.

5. Run my own business (so Faith doesn't have to be in daycare so much).

6. Write a book.

7. Make a cross-country trip to see the places I want to see.

8. Start a savings account.

9. Travel overseas (maybe see Paris?)

10. Live in a house by the beach.

After finding a job in San Diego, I could finally afford all the lessons I wanted for Faith. I also got a financial planner and began making some investments that would secure my future and provide me with money for Faith's college tuition.

I enrolled Faith in the School of Creative and Performing Arts in San Diego. She was a singing, dancing, and acting machine. She went to a school with a bigger campus than my first college!

I drove cross-country on my journey from Pennsylvania to California. It was exciting! I saw some states that I never want to return to, and some nice enough to visit again. But I was ecstatic to be living in sunny Southern California.

After several months, I left my job in the corporate world and started running a childcare program. Faith came to the program each day after school and was with me as I worked.

It wasn't my own business, but I had changed my mind

about what I wanted to do with my life. I realized that I wanted to work helping people, especially kids and teenagers. Being the director of a childcare center was close enough for me to knock number 5 off my "THINGS I WILL DO WITH MY LIFE" list.

My friend Emily and I reunited in California. She had traveled and lived an exciting ten years since graduating from high school. She was single and working on getting a career in show business. She moved in with me briefly while she was relocating to Los Angeles, and we caught up on old times. She eventually got a job working for a major network television station and moved into an apartment near Hollywood.

I also did something that wasn't on the list. I began dating someone who grew up near me in Pennsylvania. He was a single father named Bradford, who was also on a quest to make some changes in his life. Our friendship was an intense connection. We both believed in life, spirituality, and in giving more to the world than we expected back. I later married him in a small family ceremony and moved to a house two blocks from the beach, where I happily crossed number 10 off my list.

*O*ne year later, I was overjoyed to find that my husband and I were going to have a boy. Faith was happy to be getting a baby brother, and Brad, who already had one daughter in addition to Faith, was happy to be having a son.

I felt so content and blessed to have the opportunity to have this pregnancy be a little easier than the last one. Each evening, as my husband and I took long walks along the beach to exercise my pregnant body, I would say a little prayer of thanks to God. I felt blessed to have had the opportunity to make better decisions for my life, decisions that made my life and Faith's life better.

I crossed numbers 1, 2, 3, 4, 7, 8, and 9, off my list in just five years, and I couldn't believe how much my life had changed. Two years later, I had only one thing left on my list — number 6: Write a book.

I found some journals that I had written over the years, and as a sort of therapy, I began writing down the events that led me to end up in California. It was almost accidental that by the beginning of the next year, I had completed this book.

I submitted the book to a publisher called Morning Glory Press, because I had enjoyed many of their books about teen and single parenting. I couldn't believe it when they told me they liked my work and wanted to publish it.

I was very excited to cross the last item off the list I had written almost ten years earlier. I went to my desk to get the paper, but for the first time in over nine years, I could not find my list. Somewhere in the move after my marriage, I must have lost it. I looked everywhere. I tore through boxes and envelopes. I ripped through the pockets of clothing I had stored. I dumped out drawers and shelves — and I found nothing.

My husband came home after work, saw the mess I had created, and started looking for my list with me. It meant a lot to me that he understood my frustration over something as insignificant as a tattered piece of paper with my dreams written on it.

I never found that paper, and although it has irked me from time to time, I realize that it's not the paper that was important, but the journey I took. It started while I was a poor, struggling young mother, and it went to Virginia, England, Spain, France, and cross-country to California. I went from a scared girl with no job or life skills to a confident woman who isn't afraid to take risks. I grew up right alongside my child, and we somehow managed to survive my mistakes.

Recently, I went back to the restaurant where I worked before I left for college. I was shocked to see a few employees from when I was still working there. Granted, they had moved up to supervisors, but I was still surprised to see them. They asked me how my "baby girl" was, and I told them, "She's a teenager now."

It only took one second and one decision to get pregnant and change my life. That first decision I made by accident — but my decision to change things was made on purpose. Telling my old co-workers that my daughter was a teenager now made me realize how far I had come. The thought struck me that it could have been me working there in that same restaurant, wearing the same uniform for ten years. I knew I wanted more than that, and am so grateful that I made the decision when I did, so I didn't have any more years to regret.

My daughter recently told me that she was happy I was her mother because I "talk to her about stuff," and because I was always fair, even if she didn't like it. She also told me that she can't even imagine being a mother now that she's a teenager, and that she always thinks about everything we went through when people are talking about "sex and stuff" at school.

I still worry about her. I hope she can navigate her way through high school and college without too many scars, disappointments, and mistakes. I talk and talk and talk to her about life, boys, relationships, college, and money until I am blue in the face, and hope that she will have a different and easier path than I did.

That is why I wrote this book, and why I speak to other young mothers about their choices and options. I am so grateful to the lady I met a long time ago at the library story time who told me I could get financial aid to go to college. It was hearing that information that changed things for me. I hope that I, too, can provide information to single parents, information that helps them change their lives and the lives of their children.

I am only in my early thirties, and don't pretend to have all the answers. But the fact of the matter is, *you will probably struggle as a young parent.* So, if you are going to struggle either way, you may as well struggle and have a better life at the end of five or ten years. It is easier to get through nights with no money if you know that it is only temporary. That is the only thing that kept me going some days.

The formula for goal-setting I used worked for me, but will not work for everyone. Some of you may fail to achieve many of your goals using this formula, even if you are trying to work on it.

I've found three main reasons why some people accomplish goals using the list method, while others fail at it:

1. Some people hate making lists. Lists overwhelm them and make things seem tougher than "just doing" it. But if these people have a clear idea of what they want to achieve, they can also be very successful.

2. You can write down all the goals in the world, but without determination, passion, and action for a goal,

you won't achieve it. You must constantly learn, grow, be willing to take risks, and be committed to doing whatever it takes to keep moving forward. If you are distracted and indecisive, you won't reach your goal.

3. If you lack motivation or desire to change your life, several reasons might be factors. You may be overwhelmed, depressed, or feel hopeless about your situation. These feelings may be overcome by talking to someone who can identify specific reasons why you might feel this way. You may be suffering from depression and not even know it.

We, as humans, are born with a wonderful capacity for excitement and determination. Every person can find their drive and motivation *if* they choose to achieve something they are excited about, and are not being held back by hormonal, emotional, or chemical reasons.

If you have a goal and are committed to achieving it, you will. We have the ability to achieve most of the goals we set. When we fail we often lack only one thing: commitment. We think we're committed to our goal, but in reality, we're not willing to do *whatever it takes* to accomplish the objective.

The bottom line is; you can do whatever you set your mind to! So figure out what works for you and use that method. It's up to you.

No matter what your dream, whether it is college, being a singer, elevator repair person, doctor, gardener, or mechanic, you have to take action to accomplish it. Don't waste another day . . . your dreams can begin as soon as you believe in yourself, take a risk, make a plan, and *never write your goals in pencil.*

Appendix

Possible Jobs After College

Two-Year College: Associate Degree
- Medical laboratory technician • Computer technician
  - Car mechanic • Commercial artist
- Heating, air-conditioning, and refrigeration technician
  - Hotel/restaurant manager • Surveyor
    - Water-treatment plant operator
  - Registered nurse • Physical therapy assistant

Four-Year College: Bachelor's Degree
- Teacher • Computer systems analyst
  - Accountant • Artist • FBI agent
  - Graphic designer • Insurance agent
- Newscaster/sportscaster • Public relations specialist
  - Social worker • Engineer

Four-Plus Years of College: Graduate Degree
- Minister, priest, imam, or rabbi
- Scientist • Architect • Dentist • Geologist
- Lawyer • Marine biologist • Psychologist
  - Veterinarian • Zoologist • Doctor

To prepare for college, you need courses in mathematics, English, science, and history and/or geography. Ask your school counselor what courses you need to take at your school in order to be ready for college when you graduate.

GOAL SETTING LOG

Sample

My goal is to*: <u>Become a (your goal here)</u>

Week of: <u>October 10-16</u>

Things I need to find out:

    1. *How does someone become a*

    _____?

    2. *Do I have to go to school?* _____

    3. *What kind of money can I make as a*

    _____?

    4. *What kinds of places hire* _____?

    5. *Are there any physical limitations*

    stopping me from becoming a

    _____?

Where can I get answers to my questions?

    1. *Internet*

    2. *Library*

    3. *Call some schools*

Goal Setting Log

My goal is to: _____

_____

Week of _____

Things I need to find out:

1. _____

2. _____

3. _____

4. _____

5. _____

Where can I get answers to my questions?

1. _____

2. _____

3. _____

4. _____

5. _____

Things to Do This Week

My goal is to: _____

_____

Week of _____

Monday

1. _____
2. _____
3. _____
4. _____
5. _____

Tuesday

1. _____
2. _____
3. _____
4. _____
5. _____

Wednesday

1. _____
2. _____
3. _____
4. _____
5. _____

Thursday

1. _____
2. _____
3. _____
4. _____
5. _____

Friday

1. _____
2. _____
3. _____
4. _____
5. _____

Saturday/Sunday

1. _____
2. _____
3. _____
4. _____
5. _____

What I found out this week:

_____
_____
_____
_____

Decisions I made this week:

_____
_____
_____
_____

Comments:

Four-Year Colleges
with Single Parent Housing Programs

NOTE: This list is not complete. Many other colleges have housing for married or single students with children, and a childcare center onsite. However, these schools may lack the support system that many single parents need to succeed in college. Visit your local college to see if they offer a program for single parents. Many colleges and universities are finding single mothers coming out of the woodwork and insisting on an education. As a result, programs are being built each year to meet the demand.

Andrews University: GENESIS Single Parent Program
(for students over 23 years old)
Department of Behavioral Sciences
Forsyth House, Andrews University
Berrien Springs, MI 49104-0030
Toll-free: 1-800-253-2874, Phone: 616-471-6486,
Email: genesis@andrews.ed

Andrews is the best-known Adventist educational institution in the world. Andrews offers options in undergraduate, graduate and doctoral studies. If you feel like spending a year abroad, you can choose from an impressive range of opportunities at Andrews affiliate schools or serv-ice posts around the globe. The GENESIS Single Parent Program serves older single parent students by helping them reach their goal of completing an undergraduate college education. This is a tuition assistance program, but the University is committed to providing other supportive measures to assist single parent families as resources allow.

Baldwin-Wallace College: Single Parents
Reaching Out for Unassisted Tomorrows (SPROUT)
275 Eastland Road, Berea, Ohio 44017
Julie Candela, SPROUT Director, Phone: 440-826-2130

The SPROUT program is a comprehensive residential program for single parents (ages 18-23) and their children. Founded at Baldwin-Wallace in the fall of 1990, this program was created when it was identified that many single parents drop out of the college environment when it becomes difficult to care for their children. Many are unable to finance day care, independent housing, or their education, given the many competing needs. However, without a college degree most single parents (primarily women) are unable to break the cycle of welfare. Given the opportunity of campus housing and nearby day care, this cycle can be broken.

Berea College: Non-Traditional Student Support
Berea, Kentucky 40404
Phone: 859-985-3500, Toll-Free: 1-800-326-5948
Email: admissions@berea.edu

U.S. News and World Report named Berea College the best comprehensive college for a Bachelor's degree in the South for 2005. The College maintains nontraditional student housing units, operates the child development laboratory for preschool/day care purposes, and has an involved nontraditional student program run through the Office of Labor and Student Life.

This program assists nontraditional students with the transition to college life. Help is offered in obtaining social and financial support, and developing academic and life skills to better ensure continued success in and beyond life at Berea. Most nontraditional students develop strong relationships with each other, providing a support network for study groups, baby-sitting, and other areas.

College Misericordia:
Women with Children Program
301 Lake St., Dallas, PA 18612
Toll Free: 1-866-262-6363 Phone: 570-675-4449

If you are a single mother who is determined to finish your education and provide a better life for your children, College Misericordia has a special program that can help you reach your goal. The Women with Children Program is designed for academically qualified single mothers of all ages, providing them with the opportunity to attend classes while living on the Misericordia campus with their children. Participants' children must be at least two years old at the time of the mother's entrance, and no older than 12 years of age by her graduation. This program offers convenience, personal support, and financial help that can lead to confidence, academic success, and economic self-sufficiency.

College of Saint Mary
Mothers Living & Learning Program
1901 S. 72nd Street Omaha, NE 68124-2377
Toll Free: 1-800-926-5534, Phone: 402-399-2405
Email: enroll@csm.edu

College of Saint Mary is an all-women's college. Research has found that graduating from a women's college is one of the best predictors of success for women. Females who attend all-women colleges report greater satisfaction than their coed counterparts with their college experiences in almost all measures — academically, developmentally, and personally. They are more likely to graduate, tend to hold higher positions, are happier, and earn more money. The Mothers Living and Learning program is an innovative residential option for currently unmarried women with children who would like to pursue a degree while living on campus. The college provides on-campus housing year-round to single mothers and their children so that the mother can pursue a degree full-time. This program is for women who: 1. Have up to two children who are under the age of 10 by the mother's graduation year; 2. Are determined to complete their college degree in a supportive environment; 3. Are seeking a learning experience that recognizes that they have a child.

Emporia State University
1200 Commercial Street, 308 South Morse Hall
Emporia, Kansas 66801
Phone: 620-341-5267
Website: www.emporia.edu/nontrad
Email: ntctr@emporia.edu.

The Single Parent Program provides services for students who are single parents through the facilitation of need-based childcare scholarships as well as resources and support of students as they progress toward their educational goals. Applications for the childcare scholarships are available through the nontraditional student program coordinator and the financial aid office. Awards are made on an annual basis depending on funding.

Endicott College Keys to Degrees Program
376 Hale Street, Beverly, MA 01915
Website: www.endicott.edu/keystodegrees
Jill Sullivan, Director, Phone: 978-232-2011
Email: jsulliva@endicott.edu

Keys to Degrees: Educating Two Generations Together is designed for academically qualified single men and women, ages 18 to 23, who are the parents of young children. Choosing from among the college's outstanding programs of study, these young parents have the opportunity to complete an undergraduate degree in an environment that supports their special needs and the needs of their children. Program benefits include campus housing and a full array of support services offered by the College.

Saint Paul's College: Single Parent Support System (SPSS)
115 College Drive
Lawrenceville, Virginia 23868
Phone: 434-848-3111

The program at this historically Black college currently serves twenty single parent families. It is an opportunity for the continuation of education for the parents, and provides a wholesome environment for the children so that both can break the cycle of poverty. It is a system of support where single parents and their children aspire to be the best they can be by acquiring a college education. Students accepted into the SPSS must attend summer school, and are under the same code of conduct as other dormitory students. SPSS students have generally performed academically at a relatively high level.

Wilson College: Women with Children Program
1015 Philadelphia Ave, Chambersburg, PA 17201
Toll Free: 1-800-421-8402, Phone: 717-262-2536
Email: wwc@wilson.edu

Wilson College is a small, private women's college. Wilson's Women with Children program provides on-campus residential housing year-round to single mothers and their children so that the mother can pursue a Bachelor's degree full-time. Wilson College has a long tradition that focuses on the intellectual and personal development of women. Here you will find a culture where women help other women.

Why Dads Are Important
U.S. Departments of Education and Health and Human Services

Children benefit from positive involvement with their fathers.

Involvement by fathers in activities such as eating meals with their children and helping with homework is associated with fewer behavior problems, greater sociability, and better school performance by children and adolescents. Children whose fathers are involved in their child's school experience:

- Better grades.
- Lower likelihood of repeating a grade or of being expelled or suspended.
- Increased participation in extracurricular activities.
- More enjoyment of school.

Father's play is more than fun.
Fathers are more likely to promote young children's intellectual and social development through physical play, while mothers are more likely to do so through talking and teaching while caretaking. Cultural, economic, and individual circumstances also influence child-father interactions.

Fathers help children be ready to learn.
Children's educational success depends both on educators who are *ready to teach* and on ensuring that every child is *ready to learn*. From the prenatal stage through young adulthood, children benefit from having fathers and mothers engaged in keeping them safe and healthy.

Fathers are more fun at football games.
Children report that they enjoy their school and sports activities most when their fathers are highly involved. The ongoing involvement of fathers and mothers in children's learning is extremely important.

What can you do?
Be involved in your children's learning at home and at school. Take parenting classes. Go on school outings and spend evening and weekend hours with your kids. Aim for flexible work schedules in order to have time for school visits and volunteering.

How do young dads feel?
Ask your child's father to answer the following questions, and discuss the feelings he has over becoming a young dad. Often, although incorrectly, the father's feelings are not considered to be as strong as the mother's feelings.

- ☐ I have had a hard time keeping my mind on school or work since I have had a child.
- ☐ I am often depressed since becoming a parent.
- ☐ I want to see my child more.
- ☐ I have discussed the plan I have for my child with the child's mother.
- ☐ I have friends that I talk to about my feelings.
- ☐ I feel ignored by my family and friends.
- ☐ I feel overwhelmed about being a father.
- ☐ My child's mother criticizes me often.
- ☐ I talk to my child every day.
- ☐ I am afraid that I will not be a good parent.
- ☐ I tell my child that I love him/her.
- ☐ I play with my child.
- ☐ I have received a call or letter from some of my family since becoming a parent.

Annotated Bibliography

Arnoldi, Katherine. *The Amazing True Story of a Teenage Single Mom.* 1998. 176 pp. $16. Hyperion.
Written in a true experience/comic book format, it's the story of a young mom who had dreams, but faced many obstacles in fulfilling them.

Arthur, Shirley. *Surviving Teen Pregnancy: Your Choices, Dreams and Decisions.* 1996. 192 pp. $12.95. Teacher/Study Guides, $2.50/set. Morning Glory Press, 6595 San Haroldo Way, Buena Park, CA 90620. 714.828.1998, 888.612.8254.
Helps pregnant teens understand their alternatives. Offers guidance in learning decision-making. Chapters on pregnancy options are included.

Davis, Deborah. *You Look Too Young to Be a Mom: Teen Mothers Speak Out on Love, Learning, and Success.* 2004. 287 pp. $14.95. Perigee (Penguin Books).
Thirty-five women who delivered their first child as a teenager tell their stories — rather, they write about a specific part of their lives. Each is well written and intensely interesting. Book can destroy any stereotypes the reader may have about very young parents.

Earle, Janice. *Counselor/Advocates: Keeping Pregnant and Parenting Teens in School.* 1990. 47 pp. $5. National Association of State Boards of Education, 277 South Washington St., Ste. 100, Alexandria, VA 22314. 703.684.4000.
Report of a demonstration project testing the effects of using counselor/advocates to help pregnant and parenting teens stay in school. Good resource to offer administrators when you're trying to develop special services for teenage parents within the regular school.

Goyer, Tricia. *Life Interrupted: The Scoop on Being a Young Mom.*
2004. 224 pp. $9.95. Zondervan.
*Author draws on her personal experience and that of other teens facing the
reality of becoming a mother, offering hope, tips and tricks to get through
the difficult times.*

Horn, Wade F., Ph.D. *Father Facts.* Fourth Edition. 2002. 106 pp. $15.
The National Fatherhood Initiative, One Bank Street, Suite 160,
Gaithersburg, MD 20878. 301.948.0599.
*This book is filled with important facts, information, and research
concerning the plight of fatherlessness.*

Jacobs, Thomas A., et al. *What Are My Rights? 95 Questions and
Answers about Teens and the Law.* 1997. 208 pp. $14.95. Free Spirit
Publishing. 612.338.2068.
*A matter-of-fact guide to the laws that affect teens at home, at school, on the
job, and in their communities.*

Levin-Epstein, Jodie. *Teen Parent Provisions in the Personal Responsibility and Work Opportunity Reconciliation Act of 1996.* 1996. 80
pp. $7.50. Center for Law and Social Policy, CLASP Publications,
1015 15th St. NW, Ste. 400, Washington, DC 20005. 202.906.8000.
*Reviews Act and highlights restrictions on assistance to teens, incentives to
states to invest in pregnancy prevention, and other provisions of the new law
that may affect teen parents and teens at risk of early parenting.*

Leving, Jeffery M. and Kenneth A. Dachman. *Fathers' Rights: Hard-
hitting and Fair Advice for Every Father Involved in a Custody
Dispute.* 1998. 240 pp. $16. Basic Books.
*This powerful book provides accurate and authoritative information re-
garding child support and custody issues. Good for program providers.*

Lindsay, Jeanne Warren. *Do I Have a Daddy? A Story About a Single-
Parent Child.* 2000. 48 pp. Paper, $7.95; hardcover, $14.95. Free
study guide. Morning Glory Press.
*A beautiful full-color picture book for the child who has never met his/her
father. A special sixteen-page section offers suggestions to single mothers.*

_____. *Teen Dads: Rights, Responsibilities and Joys (Teens
Parenting* **Series**)*.* 2001. 224 pp. $12.95. Teacher's Guide,
Workbook, $2.50 each. Morning Glory Press.
*A how-to-parent book especially for teenage fathers. Offers help in
parenting from conception to age 3 of the child. Many quotes from and
photos of teen fathers. Other titles in this series include* **Your Pregnancy
and Newborn Journey, Nurturing Your Newborn, Your Baby's First Year,
The Challenge of Toddlers,** *and* **Discipline from Birth to Three.**

_____. *Teenage Couples — Caring, Commitment and Change: How to Build a Relationship that Lasts. Teenage Couples — Coping with Reality: Dealing with Money, In-laws, Babies and Other Details of Daily Life.* 1995. 208, 192 pp. $9.95 ea. Workbooks, $2.50 ea. Curriculum Guide, $19.95. Morning Glory Press.
Series covers such important topics as communication, handling arguments, keeping romance alive, sex in a relationship, jealousy, alcohol and drug addiction, partner abuse, and divorce, as well as the practical details of living. Lots of quotes from teenage couples.

Marecek, Mary. *Breaking Free from Partner Abuse.* 1999. 96 pp. $8.95. Quantity discount. Morning Glory Press.
Lovely edition illustrated by Jami Moffett. Underlying message is that the reader does not deserve to be hit. Simply written. Can help a young woman escape an abusive relationship.

Pollock, Sudie. *Moving On: Finding Information You Need for Living on Your Own.* 2001. 48 pp. $4.95. 25/$75. Morning Glory Press.
Fill-in guide to help young persons find information about their community, information needed for living away from parents.

Porter, Connie. *Imani All Mine.* 1999. 218 pp. $12. Houghton Miflin.
Wonderful novel about a black teen mom in the ghetto where poverty, racism, and danger are constant realities.

Reynolds, Marilyn. **True-to-Life Series from Hamilton High.** *Detour for Emmy, Baby Help.* 1993, 1998. 256, 224 pp. Paper, $8.95 each. Morning Glory Press.
*Wonderfully gripping stories about situations faced by young single parents. **Detour for Emmy** is an award-winning novel about a 15-year-old mother. In **Baby Help,** Melissa doesn't think she's abused because Rudy "only hits her when he's drinking."*

Seward, Angela. Illustrated by Donna Ferreiro. *Goodnight, Daddy.* 2001. 48 pp. Paper, $7.95; hardcover, $14.95. Morning Glory Press.
Beautiful full-color picture book shows Phoebe's excitement because of her father's visit today. She is devastated when he calls to say, "Something has come up." Book illustrates the importance of father in the life of his child.

Terr-Humen, Elizabeth, Jennifer Manlove and Kristin Moore. *Playing Catch-Up: How Children Born to Teen Mothers Fare.* 2005. $10. (Can be downloaded.) National Campaign to Prevent Teen Pregnancy, <www.teenpregnancy.org/store>
Research showing children of teenage mothers begin kindergarten with lower levels of school readiness than those born to older mothers.

Useful Web Sites for Young Moms

www.hasbooks.com
Website is devoted to empowering girls, young women, and single mothers. Hosted by Laura Haskins-Bookser.

www.morninggorypress.com
Fiction and nonfiction books, videos, and resources for pregnant and parenting teens.

www.youngmommies.com
Support, information, and a link to other young mothers in similar situations.

www.girlmom.com
Support, community, and education for young mamas.

www.storknet.com
Pregnancy and parenting web station.

Want A Kick Start To Change Your Life? Enter The Dreams To Reality Essay Contest!

The Challenge:

Read the book… then use the advice to decide: "What are my future goals?"

Dare to dream! Write an essay on what things you need to kick start the life you were meant to live. The Has-Books Company will offer prize packages valued up to $5,000 each for two contestants per year. Will you be one of them?

- Are you a budding artist who needs art supplies, information on art competitions, and perhaps a trip to Paris to get inspiration from the masters?

- Is your dream to be a personal trainer, but you can't afford to get certified, and you need to purchase enough equipment to turn your garage into a gym?

- Maybe your dream is a simple one… you want to go to college so you can have a better future.

Whatever your dream, write why you are excited about it, and how you are going to achieve it, *with or without* this prize package.

Awards: First-place entries will be published on the Has-Books website and will be awarded a specially tailored prize package that will help them reach their goals. This contest, through The Has-Books Company, will offer prize packages valued up to $5,000 each for two contestants per year.

Who Can Enter? The contest is open to individuals 13-27 years old, who have at least one child.

Judges will evaluate a submission based on the author's self-expression and intelligibility. Papers should reflect the personality of the entrant, but be sincere in content, tone, and style. Essays should be no more than 600 words, have a list of goals included, and be written in English. Each essay will be read and ranked by reviewers at <hasbooks.org> and read by at least two members of the distinguished review panel. The review panel's evaluations will be incorporated into the final decision.

The Has-Books Company will accept one entry per person. All entries should be submitted online at <www.hasbooks.org> The preferred way to enter is by using the online form; however, you may also submit the entry form information by email at <info@hasbooks.org> Essays submitted by email should be sent as an attachment to <info@hasbooks.org> The essay should be in Microsoft Word, Word Perfect, or Adobe Acrobat PDF format.

This contest is being held by The Has-Books Company, not Morning Glory Press, nor is Morning Glory Press a promoter of this contest or responsible for the content in any manner. Any questions or comments regarding the contest should be directed to The Has-Books Company, online at <www.hasbooks.com> Complete contest rules can be found there as well.

Index

About the Author

 Laura Haskins-Bookser was born in New York City in 1972. Second born daughter to an African American musician father and Puerto Rican artist mother, she claims that her love of writing was fed by the constant stream of music, art, and culture that filled her home when she was young.

A single parent for many years, she studied and traveled through Europe with her child, eventually graduating from college in 1999. During her career, Laura has been a program director for school-age and teen programs on both the east and west coasts.

She worked as a corporate trainer, teaching cross-cultural, compassionate, and crisis communication, and presented training programs for several schools and organizations including the YWCA and Harmonium, Inc. She has devoted time to working for school-based literacy programs, manned the phone for Contact Teenline crisis hotline, and has received nonviolence training from The King Center in Atlanta, Georgia. A firm believer in service to others, she promotes Dr. King's philosophy and methods of nonviolence, human relations, and service to mankind.

When Laura is not working, she enjoys spending time on the beach near her San Diego home, and traveling with her husband and children. She and her family have visited 42 states and six countries, and plan to continue traveling until they have seen each continent. Laura hosts a website: <www.hasbooks.com> which is devoted to empowering girls, young women, and single mothers. Visit the website to get more information.

ORDER FORM
Morning Glory Press
6595 San Haroldo Way, Buena Park, CA 90620
714.828.1998; 888.612.8254   Fax 714.828.2049; 888.327.4362
Contact us for complete catalog including quantity and other discounts.
Resources for Young Parents

			Price	Total
__ *Dreams to Reality*	Paper	978-1-932538-36-6	14.95	_____
__	Hardcover	978-1-932538-37-3	21.95	_____
__ *Your Pregnancy and Newborn Journey*		1-932538-00-3	12.95	_____
__ *Tu embarazo y el nacimiento del bebé*				
		978-1-932538-42-7	12.95	_____
__ *Nurturing Your Newborn*		1-932538-20-8	7.95	_____
__ *Crianza del recién nacido*		978-1-932538-39-7	7.95	_____
__ *Your Baby's First Year*		1-932538-03-8	12.95	_____
__ *El primer año del bebé*		978-1-932538-45-8	12.95	_____
__ *Discipline from Birth to Three*		1-932538-09-7	12.95	_____
__ *The Challenge of Toddlers*		1-932538-06-2	12.95	_____
__ *Teen Dads: Rights, Responsibilities and Joys*				
__		1-885356-68-4	12.95	_____
__ *Do I Have a Daddy?*		0-885356-63-3	7.95	_____
__ *Goodnight, Daddy*		1-885356-72-2	7.95	_____
__ *Pregnant? Adoption Is an Option*		1-885356-08-0	12.95	_____
__ *Surviving Teen Pregnancy*		1-885356-06-4	12.95	_____
__ *Teenage Couples: Caring, Commitment and Change*				
__		0-930934-93-8	9.95	_____
__ *Teenage Couples: Coping with Reality*		0-930934-86-5	9.95	_____
__ *Breaking Free from Partner Abuse*		1-885356-53-6	8.95	_____
__ *Moving On*		1-885356-81-1	4.95	_____

Novels by Marilyn Reynolds:

		Price	Total
__ *Love Rules*	1-885356-76-5	9.95	_____
__ *If You Loved Me*	1-885356-55-2	8.95	_____
__ *Baby Help*	1-885356-27-7	8.95	_____
__ *But What About Me?*	1-885356-10-2	8.95	_____
__ *Too Soon for Jeff*	0-930934-91-1	8.95	_____
__ *Detour for Emmy*	0-930934-76-8	8.95	_____
__ *Telling*	1-885356-03-x	8.95	_____
__ *Beyond Dreams*	1-885356-00-5	8.95	_____

TOTAL _____

Add postage: 10% of total—Min., \$3.50; 15%, Canada _____
California residents add 7.75% sales tax _____

TOTAL _____

Ask about quantity discounts, teacher, student guides.
Visa, MasterCard, and school/library purchase orders accepted.
If not satisfied, return in 15 days for refund.

NAME _____   PHONE_____

Purchase Order #_____ Card # _____/_____/_____/_____ Exp.____

ADDRESS _____